Time to listen

The experiences of children in residential and foster care

A ChildLine study

Written and researched by Sally Morris and Helen Wheatley. Edited by Barbara Lees

Foreword by Valerie Howarth

Copyright © ChildLine 1994

Published by ChildLine
Royal Mail Building
Studd Street
London N1 0QW

Registered Charity No. 1003758

ISBN 0 9524948 0 9

Cover design by Barney Stevenson

Sub-editing by Wendy Toms

Printed and bound in Great Britain by Centurion TMD, London

Contents

About ChildLine 7

Acknowledgements 10

Foreword 12

Introduction 16

PART ONE

RESEARCH FINDINGS IN ENGLAND AND WALES

INTRODUCTION 22

ABOUT THE CHILDREN 23
Characteristics of children calling the CIC Line 23
Placements 24
Problems and concerns 26
Characteristics of children interviewed face to face 27
Coming into care 28

EXPERIENCES IN RESIDENTIAL CARE 32
Bullying in residential homes 32
Sexual abuse 33
Involvement in decision-making 35
Living environment 36
Summary of residential care findings 37

EXPERIENCES IN FOSTER CARE 38
Sexual abuse in foster care 38
Physical abuse in foster care 39
Part of the family 40
Summary of foster care findings 42

SEEKING HELP WITH PROBLEMS 43
Running away 44
Managing feelings 45
Who children tell 46
Summary 49

OTHER SOURCES OF SUPPORT 50
Family contacts 50
Siblings 51
ChildLine 52
Making private telephone calls 52
Summary 53

EDUCATION AND PLANS FOR THE FUTURE 54

CONCLUSIONS 56

SUMMARY AND RECOMMENDATIONS FOR LOCAL AUTHORITIES 60
1. Reception into care 60
2. Managing problems and feelings 61
3. Child protection 61
4. Bullying in residential homes 62
5. Education 63
6. Placement considerations 64
7. Leaving care 65

IMPLICATIONS OF RESEARCH FINDINGS FOR CHILDLINE 66

PART TWO

RESEARCH FINDINGS IN SCOTLAND

INTRODUCTION	70
ANALYSIS OF CALLS TO THE LINE	71
About children calling	71
CHILDREN'S MAIN PROBLEMS	73
Being in care	74
Placement dissatisfaction	74
Sanctions	75
Runaways	75
Decision-making	76
Bullying	77
Physical abuse	78
Sexual abuse	79
Family issues	80
Access to telephones	80
Leaving care	81
Practical help and advice	81
Social and emotional support	81
Employment	82
Summary	83
FACE TO FACE INTERVIEWS WITH CHILDREN IN CARE	84
Admission into care/contact with family	84
Rights and decisions	86
Sources of support	87
Being in care	88
The future	88
Summary	89

CONCLUSIONS 89

RECOMMENDATIONS 91
1. Reception into care 92
2. Support in care 92
3. Abused children in care 93
4. Bullying 93
5. Rights and decisions 94
6. Support networks 95
7. Leaving care 95
8. Independent developments 96

BIBLIOGRAPHY 98

APPENDICES

Appendix 1 - The research approach 99
Appendix 2 - Interview schedule 102
Appendix 3 - Information leaflet for potential interviewees 108
Appendix 4 - ChildLine's confidentiality policy 110
Appendix 5 - Main problems of children in foster care in England and Wales who called the CIC Line, Oct. '92 - March '93 111
Appendix 6 - Main problems of children in residential homes in England and Wales who called the CIC Line, Oct. '92 - March '93 112
Appendix 7 - Main problems of children who called the CIC Scotland Line, Oct. '92 - March '93 113

About ChildLine

ChildLine was established in 1986 to listen to, comfort and protect children in trouble or danger. By 31st March 1994, the agency had counselled 383,952 children. All calls are free to the children – they are paid for by ChildLine.

The Charity's first objective is to answer every child's call. We have managed to answer more and more calls every year since the service was opened, and currently answer around 3,000 every day from our five centres across the UK.[1] Despite this, we know from British Telecom monitoring of our lines that many more children try to reach our counsellors, but cannot get through, because all lines are busy. Only with more funding will ChildLine be able to close the gap between call demand and our ability to respond.

ChildLine was originally conceived as a bridging service between children who were being abused and sources of help. But children themselves, calling in their tens of thousands, have defined the service they want. Some ring us once because of a crisis in their lives. They may be pregnant; they have been physically or sexually assaulted; they have suffered bereavement. Others call because they want to talk over some aspects of growing up – friendship, falling in love, sexuality, school problems. Some ring about chronic difficulties which persistently trouble them: bullying, loneliness or depression, domestic violence in their homes. Sometimes children call because they have no one else to talk to. In 1993-4 alone, 81,543 children were counselled about these and other problems and concerns.

---

1 ChildLine bases are located in:
HQ – London:
Scotland – Glasgow:
Midlands – Nottingham
North West – Manchester:
Wales/Cymru – Swansea and Rhyl

As funding permits, four further centres are planned to cover the North East, East Anglia, the South West and Northern Ireland

Our counsellors aim to listen attentively to what children say; to encourage them to explore their feelings, to think through how difficulties might be tackled; to consider how they want to proceed and the consequences of taking particular courses of action. We try, wherever appropriate, to help them to identify an adult they know and trust, in whom they could confide their problems and concerns.

Many young people find it difficult to talk about what is worrying them straightaway, and will use various means of testing the service before they feel confident enough to speak to a counsellor. Children seldom want ChildLine to rush into action; usually they will carefully guard their anonymity, and want to be in control of the counselling and referral process, if the latter is to be instituted. Very early in ChildLine's history, our counsellors learnt that attempting to intervene before a child is ready simply results in forfeiting the trust of the child, who may then never call back. So, except in situations where the child is judged to be in extreme danger, ChildLine's service is child-led and confidential to the caller.

From its beginnings, the heart of ChildLine has been its volunteer counsellors, who now number over 500. They are of all ages and from all walks of life. Volunteers receive thorough initial and ongoing training, and constant support and supervision, to enable them to offer children a service they can trust.

ChildLine is also committed to ensuring that children's voices are more widely heard, as a means of promoting changes in social policy, practice and provision relating to children. We achieve this through the powerful evidence of the children themselves, taken directly from their calls to ChildLine. This report on children in care is one example of this commitment. Among others have been the published reports on ChildLine's previous special lines, such as the Bullying Line (1991) and the Boarding School Line (1992).

Editor's note

Throughout this report, the terms 'children' and 'young people' are used, interchangeably, to indicate children up to the age of 18. We also use both the terms 'looked after' and 'in care' to denote young people in public care, living either in residential homes or in foster care.

Finally, in accordance with ChildLine's policy of confidentiality, names and other details of individual children quoted have been altered in order that they cannot be identified.

Acknowledgements

This study by ChildLine of the experiences of children living in residential homes and with foster families was researched and written by Sally Morris and Helen Wheatley and edited by Barbara Lees. It includes contributions from Valerie Howarth, Anne Houston, Hereward Harrison and Mary MacLeod.

Dr. Michael Little of the Dartington Social Research Unit acted as consultant and adviser throughout the study.

The research was overseen by an advisory group and a steering group, consisting of staff from ChildLine, Dartington Social Research Unit, the Calouste Gulbenkian Foundation, Strathclyde and Tayside Regional Councils, Who Cares? Scotland and the Scottish Child Law Centre.

Thanks are due to all the Children in Care Line counsellors and staff, particularly Patricia Walker and Diana Nicoletti, the counselling support team at ChildLine's London office, and counselling administration personnel at ChildLine Scotland.

ChildLine is also grateful for their support to the Association of Directors of Social Work in Scotland, the Association of Directors of Social Services in England and Wales and the National Foster Care Association, and to the regional councils in Scotland and the local authorities in England and Wales and their social workers, who put ChildLine's researchers in touch with young people in their care.

Above all, we thank the young people in care who agreed to be interviewed face to face and who talked so openly and frankly about their experiences.

None of this research would have been possible without financial assistance given to ChildLine by a variety of organisations and individuals. We are particularly grateful to the Calouste Gulbenkian Foundation, Strathclyde Regional Council and the Hugh Fraser Foundation for their generous funding.

Foreword

"...it gave me self-confidence to know someone was listening to me."

This report encompasses the testimony of the many children and young people who called the special line, ChildLine for Children in Care between 14th October 1992 and 31st March 1993. It is the children's own story of their lives in public care in Britain today, and the findings and recommendations have not strayed beyond what they have told us.

When ChildLine first reviewed the use made by children in care of our main 0800 1111 number, we found them to be among the most troubled and unhappy children to whom we have talked, and among the most isolated and alone. This image has been reinforced by the children who have subsequently called the special line. They have described to our counsellors a story of family dislocation, abuse and several care placements, often reciting their histories as if from a case record. A constant theme in their conversation has been their sense of abandonment, unimportance and low self-esteem.

Throughout this project, ChildLine has been at pains to avoid raising the anxieties or defences of carers of children. The service and the study are aimed at improving the lot of children, not harassing those who care for them. Many of us at ChildLine have been carers and social workers to children in care; we know from experience that the kind of suffering these children have lived through does not predispose them to be happy, relaxed and easy. Caring for children who are so troubled would be demanding and challenging even if it were not undertaken against a background of frequent organisational, policy and legal changes, and if all the resources for the support of carers were in place.

Although the problems described by the young people showed considerable complexity, many of the solutions are simple, straightforward and readily applicable. We frequently heard that, despite all the emphasis on planning for children in care following the impact of 'drift' on children *(Rowe and Lambert)*, many children had minimal say in decision-making, and little or no preparation for, and support through, the process of achieving independence. Perhaps the most disappointing finding of all was that so many children in the study were unclear about why they had come into care. And this is despite 30 years of professional understanding of the nature of the emotional crisis for children of entry into care - however right the decision might be. *(Stevenson 1968; Department of Health and Social Security, 1985; Department of Health, 1989)*

☆   ☆   ☆

But we also found that some young people, already carrying with them a history of troubles on entering care, are subject to abuse from carers, fellow residents and foster carers. Others are again abused when visiting their families where the original abuse took place. While we are not talking about an epidemic of physical and sexual abuse and bullying, nevertheless as a proportion of all complaints voiced by children in this study, the percentage alleging abuse constituted a significant minority. It is appalling that these miseries happen to children supposedly being protected, and it is imperative that effective steps are taken to prevent such abuse occurring.

A particular cause for concern was the indication from our callers that children in foster care seem more likely to be the targets of both sexual and physical abuse than children in residential homes, particularly if they have previously been abused. In the case of some children, there was every indication that male foster carers, or other male members of the household, had planned the abuse, in at least two cases exploiting their knowledge that the children had been previously abused.

Perhaps the most prevalent problems described to us by the children were their loneliness, their feeling of being unloved and often unlovable, their perception of being somehow "personally" responsible for their situation, that they must cope as best they could because they could not identify anyone in whom to put their trust.

This isolation was reflected in what was heard from around one third of the children interviewed by our researchers or who talked to our counsellors. They described times of emotional turmoil with which they felt they had to cope on their own. The resulting manifestations of negative behaviour might have been alleviated had children not been left with such a sense of bewilderment, grief, pain, loss and anger. Some suffered bouts of depression, some inflicted wounds on themselves, some felt suicidal.

Over and over again, children said that they could not confide their concerns to their carers or social workers because they did not see them, or they were not taken seriously, or their carers simply did not have time to listen. But when they did, it made a real difference - like the child who said of a social worker: "She was really good. She gave you good advice and I felt like there was someone on my side that was willing to help me and, you know, show me the right directions."

There now exists a considerable body of research about children in care which demands to be better known and better used if we are in any way to make up for the losses already experienced by them. In the past few years, there has also been an avalanche of reports and inquiries, giving rise to guidance, advice and procedural stricture, from both government and campaigning agencies, to carers, social workers and local authorities.

It would be good to be able to say that, as a result of all this, things have markedly improved for children in care. Sadly, our study reveals how little this appears to be the case, at least for many children. Our reason for adding to the avalanche is that we believe the children who call ChildLine have given us something distinct to say about the nature of their need and how to meet it. Our primary purpose is to stress what still needs to be done, but for obvious reasons, we have not held back from making again recommendations which have been made many times before.

Children have told us what they want by way of help and support. They place enormous stress on their need and wish to have their emotional wellbeing attended to, but not in ways that they experience as being 'done to'. They want to be involved in both day to day and longer term planning, in ways which allow them to retain some feeling of being in charge of their own lives. They wish to be protected from abuse, but if they are being abused, they want to have some control over measures taken to stop the abuse and offer them protection. In residential homes, protection from other residents is a priority and they want, among other possible options, the freedom to change placements, or their key worker.

They strongly resent their confidences being broken on the basis that because they are in public care, personal information about them is public, too – to be passed around often without their knowledge or consent. In this, they simply express a basic human need – and right. But, in addition, children in care, like adults and other children, may need access to other sources of private and confidential help. It ought to be a priority for local authorities and others to set about meeting this need in ways that children are prepared to take up.

Children in care tell us simply that they are individuals who wish to be cared for, protected, respected and encouraged. We hope this study will inspire their carers, social service managers and policy-makers to continue striving towards the fulfilment of these needs. We know that the best care in the system does provide all this; it must become the norm. What matters most is someone having the time, someone having the will to listen to a child, when that child needs to be heard.

Valerie Howarth
Executive Director
ChildLine

Introduction

ChildLine established its special line for children in care (0800 88 44 44) in 1992, following a review of the use that these children had made of the main (0800 1111) number. The review was undertaken in order to make detailed submissions to the Utting (1991) and Warner (1992) commissions of inquiry into residential care, which were set up as a result of the crisis of confidence in the care system following the Beck and 'pin down' scandals.

ChildLine sought to raise funds from government and private sources to set up, publicise and research the special helpline. In the event, two anonymous donors made it possible to establish and maintain the Line for a period of five months, and the Calouste Gulbenkian and Hugh Fraser Foundations committed themselves to supporting the research in England/Wales and Scotland, respectively.

Though the line was originally planned as a six-month project, analysis of the use of the service convinced ChildLine Trustees and staff of the need to continue it indefinitely. It has been maintained ever since, thanks to generous donations from the Variety Club of Great Britain, Marks and Spencer and Strathclyde Regional Council.

In order to publicise the helpline, ChildLine wrote to all local authorities and voluntary agencies caring for children, describing the service and asking for their help. The responses, which were almost universally positive, enabled ChildLine to set up an extensive database of residential units for children.

In England and Wales, posters and leaflets were sent to all residential units on the database, and to each department's fostering section, to try to reach children in foster care. The National Foster Care Association enthusiastically supported the project and mailed ChildLine publicity material to their members. In Scotland, discussions took place with all regional councils, which then distributed posters and leaflets to their residential units and foster carers. Direct mailing was undertaken to voluntary organisations and privately-run establishments. Who Cares? Scotland and the UK organisation, Who Cares? also gave the Line a great deal of coverage in their newsletters to children in care.

This exercise was repeated nine months later to publicise the continuation of the Line.

It was clear from the start that the special counselling service to children in care, though national like the 0800 1111 line, should be offered separately to Scottish children by the ChildLine Scotland base, because the entire legal framework of child care services in Scotland is different from that in England and Wales.

We used the same title, telephone number (0800 88 44 44), leaflets and posters, so that the service had a clear UK-wide identity and could benefit from both UK and Scottish media coverage. Media interest and coverage of the press conferences launching the service were much more extensive in Scotland than in England and Wales. This signal that the public care of children may have different significance across the nation is also suggested in the differing results of the study.

Two separate studies

Delivering the service from both ChildLine's HQ and Scottish centres made it possible to analyse the results separately and compare the two systems. Part 1 of this report sets out the findings of the study in England and Wales, Part 2, the Scottish findings. There is evidence to suggest that, at least in some respects, children in care in Scotland may be better served by the care system there, than their counterparts in England and Wales. If this is the case, and it does merit further study, then factors at work in Scotland are likely to be the Children's Hearing system[2], and apparent closer co-operation there between regional authorities and the voluntary child care agencies, like Who Cares? Scotland.

Unfortunately, we were unable to undertake a separate analysis of children calling from Northern Ireland, where the legal framework also differs,

[2] Children in Scotland who commit offences or are in need of care and protection are referred to a Children's Hearing. This is a Panel of lay members, advised by a legal officer called a Reporter. The Reporter decides whether a child should appear before a panel. If the child or the child's parents disagree, the matter is referred to the Sheriff Court for proof and returned to the Panel for decisions which are in the best interests of the child.

though callers identifying themselves as being from the Province were included in the study. They were not, in fact, a large enough group from which to deduce anything distinctive about the experience of being in care in Northern Ireland. Indeed the stories were markedly similar to those of other children calling the Line at ChildLine's London headquarters.

Ever since their inception, the Children in Care lines have been staffed by experienced and sessional counsellors, who undertake training to familiarise themselves with the statutory framework of the care system, the resources available to help children, and the issues which children are likely to bring. They are constantly supported and supervised by ChildLine supervisory staff. In essence, the children ringing ChildLine for Children in Care receive the same service as those ringing the core service. The main difference is that it is easier for children to get through to the Children in Care Line.

Children still call the line

Children continue to call the ChildLine for Children in Care number, so this detailed study of 676 children who were counselled by ChildLine should be seen against the backdrop of the prevailing use of the line.

In the year following the end of the period studied, a further 508 children in care were counselled. During this period, the counselling work developed into much more ongoing work with callers. Two thirds of counsellors' time is in fact currently devoted to ongoing work, and one third to 'new' callers.

The profile of current callers to the Line is very much the same as that of the young people who formed the basis of the study. In Scotland, 20 per cent of those who specified a placement were in foster care and 70 per cent in residential care, while in England and Wales 27 per cent were fostered and 67 per cent in residential care. The most common age group spanned 14 to 16 years in both areas. Seventy eight per cent of the callers to the London base were female and 57 per cent in Scotland. And the profile of concerns was very similar to those studied for this report. The most prevalent were: being in care, bullying, current and past physical and sexual abuse, family relationship problems and running away.

In addition, for the 18 months from the onset of the study to the end of March 1994, 1711 children, identifying themselves as currently or previously in care, called ChildLine's main 0800 1111 number, rather than the CIC special Line. In all, therefore, 2219 other children in care have talked to ChildLine and, from what they have told us, there is no indication that the 676 children studied for this report were in any way dissimilar.

We began Childline for Children in Care to contribute to the wellbeing of children in care. We have learnt from this study some lessons for ourselves about how we should make ChildLine more accessible and useful to the children who call, and these are set out alongside recommendations for carers, managers and policy-makers. If only one thing is taken from this document, it should be the absolute necessity for us all to combine in finding ways which enable children to be heard.

PART ONE

Research findings in England and Wales

Research findings in England and Wales

Introduction

In this section, we report on calls made by 539 children in England and Wales to the ChildLine for Children In Care (CIC Line) in the first six months of its operation, plus face to face interviews with 46 children who were being looked after by seven local authorities in England and Wales.

The research presents a snapshot of the child's view of the care system. Since a substantial portion of the information is taken from calls made to the special CIC Line, the findings are inevitably problem-focused. Nevertheless, some children calling the Line, and some who were interviewed face to face, indicated positive aspects of the care system, and these have been included.

The face to face interviews with young people currently in care aimed to broaden the base of information and provide a context to the information emerging from the special CIC Line.

In assessing the following research findings it is important to remember the context of the research activity. The majority of the information analysed derives from records of counselling. The primary aim of ChildLine's service is to counsel children, and it is our policy that counselling will be 'child-led'. It follows that some questions useful for research purposes will not necessarily be put to the child. As a result, in several of the areas analysed there will be an unusually high proportion of 'no data' responses. Despite this, the counselling records provide a rich source of information for research, and recording systems have been specially developed which facilitate research activity.

About the children

Since the information in the report is based on counselling records and interviews with children currently in local authority care throughout England and Wales, it is important to examine the extent to which the characteristics of this group reflect those of the general population of children in public care. The following information describes what we know about the children and where they were living.

Characteristics of children calling the CIC Line

Most of the 539 callers were female (76%) and over half (53%) were aged between 14 and 16. The youngest caller was seven. This pattern reflects ChildLine's other services, which are used mainly by girls in their middle teens and are unlikely to receive calls from under-fives. The children calling the CIC Line were older than the typical "looked-after" child, and nearly one in ten was 18 and therefore about to leave care.

The table below shows the age distribution of callers to the CIC Line, compared with the national population of children looked after by local authorities.

TABLE 1

	Using ChildLine's CIC Line	Looked after in England and Wales*
Under 5 years	Nil	17%
5 - 9 years	2%	22%
10 - 15 years	69%	39%
16 - 17 years	21%	21%
Over 17 years	8%	1%
	100%	100%

*Source: Dartington Social Research Unit (1994)

By far the biggest difference between children calling the CIC Line and others in foster or residential care was gender. Three quarters of those telephoning the service were female while more young people being looked after by local authorities are male. Only eight of the children counselled indicated that they were from a minority ethnic group, and this information only came to light because it had a direct bearing on their reason for calling the service (for example, racist bullying). Only one of the children calling reported having a disability. There is no way of knowing what proportion of other children calling the line also had these characteristics.

Placements

Of the children who called the CIC Line, 95 per cent indicated the type of placement they were in. Just over half (54%) were in a residential children's home, nearly a third (32%) were from foster placements. This is a reverse of the pattern for all children looked after in England and Wales, where more children are in foster placements. This fact suggests either that children in residential care had more information about the service, or were more likely to use it. The remainder were mainly children in homes with education on site, in secure accommodation, therapeutic units and other specialist provision.

A third of those using the Line had been away from home for six months or less, and were highly likely to be returning to relatives in the near future. At the other end of the scale, over two-fifths had been looked after for three or more years. The comparison by length of stay can be seen in the following table.

TABLE 2

	Using ChildLine's CIC	Looked after in England and Wales*
Looked after for:		
1 - 6 months	33%	17%
7 - 12 months	9%	12%
13 - 24 months	14%	29%
25 - 60 months	24%	15%
> 61 months	20%	27%
	100%	100%

*Source: Dartington Social Research Unit (1994)

Half the children counselled discussed previous care placements. Most of these had experienced relatively few placement changes; 39 per cent had changed placements once. Nevertheless, 26 per cent had experience of four or more placements.

Of children calling the Line, 347 children (64%) gave some indication of why they thought they were in care; a further two per cent specifically said they did not know why. Children reported a wide range of problems as the reason for their being away from home; the largest group were experiencing physical (25%) or sexual abuse (21%). This is in contrast to the position nationally where most of the children in care or accommodated are there as a result of other family problems.

Twenty per cent of those who spoke about it mentioned 'other' reasons, many of which could not in themselves have precipitated care proceedings or a voluntary reception - for example. "I stole 10p from my Mum"; "I wanted to go to a children's home". Seven of these 'other' children referred to some form of abuse, but were not able to expand on it. Two others indicated they had asked to be taken into care.

Children calling the CIC Line do not seem to be typical of all looked after children in terms of their legal status. Information from just over a quarter of the children who called showed that more were separated by voluntary arrangements while children subject to other court orders were under-represented. However, the confusion some children have about their legal status is in itself a concern.

Two thirds of callers identified the region from which they were calling. Calls were made from all over the country. It was not surprising to find that the Line received more calls from densely populated regions of England and Wales. Nevertheless, there was some indication that certain regions may have made particular efforts to distribute information about the Line.

Eighty-eight per cent of children calling the CIC Line indicated the site of the telephone they were using. Forty one per cent 'phoned from a telephone box. Further analysis revealed that children in foster care were much less likely to use a telephone in their placement than those in residential care. Thirty-four per cent of children known to be in a children's home called from a telephone in their home, compared with only 13 per cent in foster placements; and 40 per cent of children in foster care used a public telephone compared with 36 per cent of children in residential homes.

Problems and concerns

Children called the CIC Line with a variety of problems and concerns. In most cases their experiences before coming into care and during their stay in care meant that they had multiple problems. Nevertheless, children called the CIC Line usually to seek help and support in dealing with a specific issue. The main problems presented by children in foster care were generally quite different from those in residential care, and there were also significant differences between male and female callers. The following sections explore these differences in more detail. The diagram below shows the general range of problems that children called about, and the most common concerns that they presented.

Characteristics of children interviewed face to face

Forty-six children were interviewed face to face in seven local authority areas in England and Wales. They were mainly young people in children's homes or in foster care. Eleven of the children interviewed were accommodated in homes with education on site. Four of the older children were living in semi-independent residential units. Overall there were 22 children in foster care and 24 in residential placements. Just over half (54%) of the children said they were in long-term placements. Table 3 summarises who the children were and where they were living:

TABLE 3

CHILDREN AND YOUNG PEOPLE INTERVIEWED FACE TO FACE		
IN FOSTER CARE		
Age band	MALE	FEMALE
10 - 12 yrs	4	4
13 - 15 yrs	6	4
16 - 18 yrs	1	3
Totals	11	11
IN RESIDENTIAL CARE		
Age band	MALE	FEMALE
10 - 12 yrs	2	0
13 - 15 yrs	9	5
16 - 18 yrs	4	4
Totals	15	9

As the table shows, most of the children were aged between 13 and 15 yrs. The youngest child interviewed was ten while the oldest was 18. Eight of the children described themselves variously as mixed race, black or Asian.

Geographically, children were located in both rural and urban areas. They were distributed through England and Wales in the following way:

TABLE 4

AREA OF THE COUNTRY	Number of Children
Northern England	10
Midlands	16
Southern England	8
Wales	12
Total	46

Forty one per cent of the children interviewed were in care because of family relationship problems. A further 26 per cent had been separated from their families as a result of physical or sexual abuse. Twenty two per cent of the children interviewed had been in care for less than a year but most had been living in care for much longer periods; 37 per cent for over five years.

Coming into care

Louise (16) was asked during interview about why she was in care. She responded by describing the process of coming into care at the age of 14:

> "I felt so isolated from them all. I'd had a barney with my sister. I felt my sister was favoured 'cause of all her ailments and things. I felt I was getting complementary rewards for acts and she would get rewards for existing.
>
> "Anyway we'd (she and her mother) had a physical fight. She had hit me and I hit back and then I had to stay in my room and I tried to come down for something to eat and me Mum gave me such a mouthful and made me feel so horrible. I can't really understand why she was angry 'cause I can't really understand why I was angry. I think she was really angry with herself and her life really.
>
> "It was like three days over the holiday, then I had to go back to school and I'd gone to go out of the house and me Dad stopped me (he's my step-dad but he's always been the father figure) and he said, 'Where are you going?' I was beyond caring then and just about to have a go. I says, 'I was going to school,' and then he said, 'Well, I don't think you should, your Mum's just gone down to the 'phone box to phone social services. You might have to stay with them.' And because we'd had like a physical fight, the following day my Mum had taken me down to the doctor's. So anyway, I don't know how it was but I went to school and on the way I got to a 'phone box and phoned my two best friends."

At school her sister had spoken to a friend about the argument between Louise and her mother. Word soon spread and later her sister heard that Louise had been saying she was abused by her mother. Louise said she had not said this to anyone and feels it was just gossip that her sister had started, heard back and later relayed to their mother as coming from Louise.

She described how her mother came up to the school gates at lunch time and shouted at her, saying, "I've been abusing you have I, well you're not coming back then, see how you like that." Louise described how embarrassed she felt by her mother ranting at her in front of the other children and how this had prevented her from countering her mother's accusations.

Louise was shocked when a teacher called her in to discuss events at home, but she was still upset by what had happened and was grateful for an opportunity to talk it through and cry about what had happened. It was only later that she realised that she really was not going to return home that evening.

Later that day Louise was told by the teacher that her mother had refused to have her home and she would be taken to a temporary home for the evening. So Louise entered a foster care placement that evening. She has remained in foster care ever since and has had very little contact with her family since these events.

Louise typifies the response children gave when they were asked about why they thought they were in care. During interviews children commonly described the series of events leading up to their being taken into care. Others were unable to answer the question, either because they had no real idea of why they were in care (these were often children who had come into care at an early age) or because the emotion of that time had been overwhelming and remained so.

In trying to explain their current situation, children who were interviewed grasped hopelessly at the events preceding separation, indicating that maybe it was some small thing that they had done, or some unknown fact about a parent or themselves which had caused social workers to "take them away from home". Many of the reasons children gave during interview and on the CIC Line were implausible explanations on their own: for example, "Mum has a busy job", "Being naughty at school".

Generally the interviews suggested that the younger children were when they came into public care, the more confused they were likely to be about the reasons why they were there. Children who were in care for family relationship problems were often particularly unclear about why they were being looked after. This was especially true of those children whose siblings had remained at home. When children did recall the first time they were separated from their family they often had difficulty talking about these experiences.

Over a third (34%) of children calling ChildLine for Children in Care did not directly refer to the reason why they were in the care system. Of those who did, the largest group were being looked after because of experiences of sexual or physical abuse (46%). Twenty per cent of children gave other explanations. These were often vague but generally suggested family relationships - for instance, "Mother does not want me", "I was naughty/badly behaved", or parents arguing. Two of these children had asked to be taken into care.

Children expressed a variety of emotions about their experience of coming into care. Fear, loss, guilt and anger were the most common. Louise, in the example above, began to cry, recalling these events. She said: "I can't describe the feeling, ..oh just pure loss." The majority said it was a time of great confusion and sadness.

Around one fifth of the children interviewed and 17 per cent of those who spoke about it on the CIC Line either did not know or were confused about why they were in the care system. The consistent exceptions were those children who had been physically and sexually abused at home. Similarly very few of the children knew their legal status, or what rights they had once they were being looked after by the local authority.

Children who were uncertain about why they were in care described how they had received little or no information from their social workers. Louise said that her social worker treated her like a naughty girl that day and made her feel totally responsible for her situation. Few had been given the opportunity to discuss the reasons or the process of coming into care with their parents or indeed with their carers. Siblings and friends had occasionally been more supportive, but some children found that their siblings in particular had different understandings of why they were there.

Summary

Generally these findings suggest that for a substantial group of children in England and Wales, the process of coming into care was characterised by a lack of information on why they were removed from home. This seemed to exacerbate and prolong the grief they felt on being separated from their families. Interestingly, this finding is not evident from the analysis of information on Scotland. Whatever the explanation, children described being haunted by this gap in their personal history and many had strong feelings of guilt or anger, often associated with fantasy explanations for being in care.

Coming into care was often the most sensitive area discussed with children; they commonly broke down and wept at this point. Many still felt emotionally vulnerable recalling these experiences, even though the events were often years in the past.

This response indicated that many children generally required further support to come to terms with their feelings about leaving their families and coming into public care. Those children who remain confused about why they are being looked after would undoubtedly benefit from additional information on the reasons for their removal, as well as opportunities to talk about how they felt about the separation.

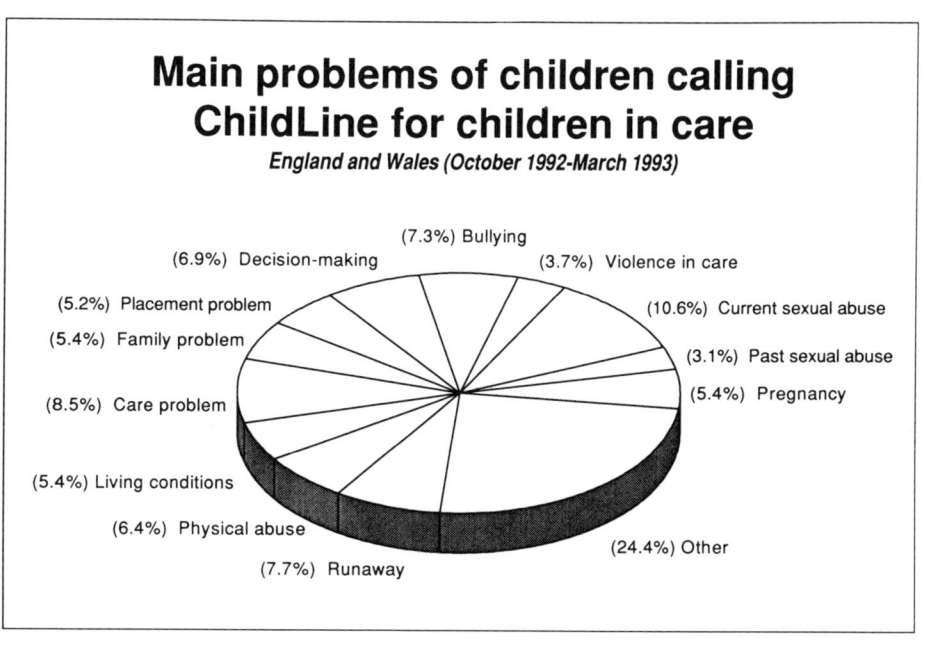

Main problems of children calling ChildLine for children in care
England and Wales (October 1992-March 1993)

- (7.3%) Bullying
- (6.9%) Decision-making
- (3.7%) Violence in care
- (5.2%) Placement problem
- (10.6%) Current sexual abuse
- (5.4%) Family problem
- (3.1%) Past sexual abuse
- (8.5%) Care problem
- (5.4%) Pregnancy
- (5.4%) Living conditions
- (6.4%) Physical abuse
- (24.4%) Other
- (7.7%) Runaway

Experiences in residential care

Of the callers to the CIC Line, 278 said they were in residential care and 75 per cent of these were girls. Generally, residential care placements seemed to raise a quite different range of problems from those of foster care.

The living environment provided in residential placements was often a source of discomfort for children. Living with a group of children from diverse and troubled backgrounds could be very stressful. During interview, children also commonly described having to become 'tougher' and more self-reliant in order to survive these pressures.

Children calling the CIC Line from residential care indicated a variety of problems (see Appendix 6). Overall, the main problems related to bullying in the home (10%), current sexual abuse (9%), and specific problems with living conditions and/or other aspects of their placements (8%). However, there were significant gender differences; most boys (20%) called about bullying, while the most common problem among girls was current sexual abuse (9%).

Bullying in residential homes

Over a quarter of the boys (18 children) and 11 per cent (24) of the girls who said they were in residential placements called the CIC Line about a problem of bullying or violence from other residents. The prevalence of this problem was confirmed during interviews with children who had experience of residential care, and is consistent with previous research by Whitaker and her colleagues (1991) who made detailed observations of relationships between children in four residential children's homes.

Girls calling the CIC Line were more likely to describe physical attacks from other residents as 'violence' while boys referred to them as 'bullying'. Overall, boys in residential homes were more likely to be involved in bullying, both as perpetrators and victims.

Bullying in children's homes covered a range of behaviour, from persistent teasing or being 'picked on' to physical attacks. Not surprisingly, group bullying was much more prevalent in residential homes, but was not a problem confined to large homes. Children described being teased about their race, culture, body size and, in some cases, their reason for being in care - for instance, the death of a parent. Violent bullying was more often perpetrated by boys and was likely to be a result of an argument between two individuals, or a group of children intimidating others in the home.

The interviews suggested that communal living, with children from a diverse range of backgrounds, could be a source of tension. Children discussed how other children in the home would 'wind them up' or tease them. Children's coping responses to this form of behaviour included trying to ignore it, creating firm boundaries with the offenders so that they could feel untouched by it, or responding with similar jibes and teasing. Some felt that every so often it was inevitable that an argument or physical fight would erupt to release the tension between residents. As Helen, a 15-year-old in residential care described one such occasion:

> "Sometimes we fall out, like I get wound up a lot in this place. Like Patrick, (another resident) he winds me up too many times. One of the staff said to him, 'One of these days you're going to get a slap from the kids, winding them up like that.' "So I thought, right, like one time he was winding me up, so I slapped him and I goes, 'You asked for that, Patrick.'

Children calling the line with problems of bullying or violence from other children had generally told staff about their problems but most felt their concerns had been ignored. Children reported being told to ignore the teasing or name-calling. Similarly, physical fights were usually out of the sight of staff, who seemed reluctant to take action on the accounts of children alone. Withdrawing from interactions with other residents or requesting a placement change were usually last resort attempts by children to avoid persistent bullying. Some felt they had no place of refuge in the home.

Sexual abuse

Allegations of current sexual abuse were made by 25 children - nine per cent of those known to be in residential care. Another 12 children (4% of those known to be in residential care) called with problems centred on past sexual abuse. Overall, this represented 15 per cent of the girls known to be in residential care and nine per cent of the boys.

The main perpetrators of current sexual abuse in residential care were reported to be male residents in nine cases and male residential staff in eight cases. Most of the remainder were children who had been abused on home visits. Staff and residents generally perpetrated the abuse in the home during the evening. A common scenario was described by Abby, a 13-year-old girl who had been taken into care as a result of sexual abuse by her stepfather.

> Abby reported that one of the male staff at the home would come into her room at night or call her into the office and lock the door. She said that he "kisses and touches her" and makes her touch him and it was getting worse each time. She felt she couldn't go to sleep and was frightened to disclose the abuse because he had threatened to kill her.

Children described how powerless they felt to stop the abuse, particularly when the abuser was their key worker (as in three cases). Several children had been threatened with physical abuse (and in three cases death) if they told about the abuse. Others had been threatened with moves to secure accommodation. Children were more likely to have told about abuse by another resident, but most were simply not believed.

Children calling about past sexual abuse were more highly represented in residential placements than other forms of placement. Children described difficulties in finding the opportunity to talk confidentially about their past abuse. The interviews confirmed this finding. Two thirds of the children who called CIC about past sexual abuse had been taken into care as a result of this abuse. The remainder were in care for other reasons. Some had yet to disclose their sexual abuse. Many of these children were experiencing difficulties in their relations with others, of relating to and particularly trusting other people enough to develop close relationships. These problems invariably led children to feel hopeless, isolated or depressed. Some talked of suicidal thoughts and deliberately harming themselves.

Most of the children who called with a problem of sexual abuse (past or current) felt isolated with their problem. Some complained that the residential placement offered them little privacy or few opportunities to talk confidentially. Generally they were experiencing strong emotions and felt unable to manage or come to terms with these feelings.

Although the information from the Line suggests current sexual abuse is less of a problem for children in residential care than for those in foster care, the experience of being abused within a residential community can leave the child feeling just as isolated. Children who have come into care with past experiences of sexual abuse can become a target for further abuse in this environment. The number of male children involved in abusive relationships with other children in residential homes is disturbing. So is the fact that when children report this form of abuse they are likely to be met with disbelief. Two of the children calling the CIC Line suggested that staff in the home thought the abuser was their boyfriend and were unlikely to suspect them as abusers. Others said the young abuser was 'normally very quiet' or 'well-liked' and they felt they wouldn't be believed if they told.

From children's accounts, residential homes seemed to provide few opportunities for children to talk through their feelings about past abuse and the same may also be true for children who are experiencing current abuse. The absence of an intimate confidant may partly be a result of the abuse itself, but children described staff as being unavailable and difficult to approach about such personal matters. Some children had little or no confidence in their key worker. Some of the girls felt it was inappropriate that they should have been allocated a male worker in view of their past experiences of abuse. Others felt they simply had nothing in common with their key workers, or found it difficult to talk to them.

Involvement in decision-making

Other major concerns for children living in residential homes usually centred on particular aspects of life in the placement. Despite the important principle of working in partnership established in the regulations and guidance to the Children Act, 14 (6%) of the children known to be in residential care called the CIC Line with dissatisfaction about the process and/or the outcome of decisions made on their behalf. For example:

> Robin called the CIC Line about the fact that he had been given two weeks' notice that his residential home was to be closed. The children had not been consulted about the decision and he had no information about where he was going to be moved to. Robin said, "It's my home. They can't just shut it.."

Other children who had been asked to contribute their views and opinions to the decision-making process called to complain that these had been ignored. Interviewees also suggested that children's views had less weight

than those of social workers and residential carers, notably when the child wanted:
- a change of placement
- access to siblings or parents
- not to return home
- to move to a more independent living environment

These children were left feeling they had little control over their lives. They were commonly older children (over 15 years of age) who could normally expect to be taking some responsibility for decisions about their lives. They felt unheard and resentful at the inadequacies of the system which allowed their views to be overlooked or ultimately overridden.

As Dan, an 18-year-old in semi-independent living accommodation reported during an interview:

> "They listened but at the end of the day, it's their decision. They always said, 'You've got to be in a meeting, otherwise we won't know how you feel, and you've got to be there to voice your opinion, how you feel.' I always go to the meetings and it's always their decision, they always have the last say, whatever."

Living environment

Another area of concern for children in residential care was the living environment. Children commonly described a lack of privacy, particularly because of communal bathrooms and shared rooms. They were concerned that they had little or no space to be alone or free from interruptions from staff and other residents. This was most likely to be a problem for children who had previous experience of personal space at home with their family, and those who were attempting to study at the residential home. Others felt they were unable to 'own' such personal space as they had, because of restrictions limiting (or in some cases prohibiting) the use of wall space - for instance, for displaying decorative pictures or posters.

The food provided in residential homes was also mentioned by a number of children, both during face to face interviews and on the special Children in Care Line. Children felt that the catering did not reflect their tastes or needs. Vegetarian children complained that they generally had a very limited diet and that their choice not to eat meat was often a source of ridicule from staff cooking food in the homes.

Generally, and not surprisingly, children living in smaller residential units (of up to ten residents) with a relatively stable team of staff and group of residents, were much happier in their placements. These children were better able to identify with their residential home and felt closer both to the staff and residents with whom they lived.

> Neil had previously lived in several large residential homes. At the time of his interview, he had recently moved to a small residential unit with ten children. He said: "It's better here than other places. I think the best thing is there's a lot of staff, so you get lots of attention. Before this I was in a home where there were a lot more kids and fewer staff. It just wasn't enough, 'cause if you wanted to talk to someone, it was difficult."

Summary of residential care findings.

Children in residential homes experience a range of problems associated with their communal living environment. Bullying and violence from other residents seem to be particularly difficult problems to resolve in residential units. Many of the children had complained to staff but the bullying had continued. Bullying often took the form of groups of children, usually boys, intimidating other residents, often in a violent way.

Children in residential care commonly reported dissatisfaction with their living environment, meals, and the facilities available to them. They were also more likely to complain of not being listened to or valued when decisions were being made which affected their lives.

A significant proportion of girls called from residential care about problems relating to current and past sexual abuse. Male staff and residents were the main perpetrators of the current abuse. Problems of coming to terms with past sexual abuse were also more prevalent in residential homes.

The findings suggest that children have fewer opportunities to discuss intimate problems, such as past abuse, in residential care.

Experiences in foster care

Twenty two (48%) of the children interviewed face to face and 162 (nearly a third) of the children calling the CIC Line were in foster care. Children in foster care called the CIC Line with a variety of problems (see Appendix 5) connected with current placements, abuse – past and present – and the difficulties of becoming an adult. Interestingly, the problems most often raised by girls in foster placements were not shared by the boys. On the CIC Line girls were most likely to call with problems of abuse, physical and sexual; boys called most commonly about problems connected with living conditions or decision-making in the foster home.

Sexual abuse in foster care

The CIC Line received a disturbing number of reports of current sexual and physical abuse in foster care. Twenty four of the children known to be in foster care (15%) reported being sexually abused and 20 (12%) said they were physically abused. Twenty three of the 24 young people reporting current sexual abuse were girls who were being abused in their foster placement. Two common scenarios emerge from their accounts. The example of Juliette demonstrates one of these:

> Juliette (15) had been in her foster placement for two years. She said of her foster parents: "..being with them is like being on a different planet, I am with people who love me instead of hating me.". They had recently re-fitted her bedroom, and had given her a TV and video. Juliette reported that for the last six months their own son (17) had been coming into her bedroom when her foster parents were out. He had been sexually abusing her, which she said "..is hurting me physically and mentally". She was reluctant to disclose the abuse because she did not want to lose her foster parents. Before ringing ChildLine she had contemplated suicide.

Foster brothers were the most common perpetrators of sexual abuse reported on the line, accounting for 11 of the 24 cases in foster care. All were the 'natural' child of the foster carer(s). The victims of this abuse were all girls aged between 15 and 17 years. A significant factor seemed to be the age difference between the predominantly male abusers and the foster child; the abusers were commonly two or three years older.

There were also children who were being abused by a foster father figure, either a live-in partner or a boyfriend regularly visiting the house. These children were generally younger (11 - 13 years) than those being abused by other children. The children described foster father figures who abused them while the foster mother was out or working. Most had been subjected to strong threats which inhibited their ability to talk about the abuse. In two cases the abuse had started with the foster fathers asking the children about their previous experiences of sexual abuse, and both children were initially asked to re-enact previous abuse.

Both of the above groups of children were more likely to be in longer-term foster placements. Four of the children were being looked after by the local authority because of previous sexual abuse. Some of the girls interviewed had previous experience of sexual abuse both at home and in other placements. Three of the girls interviewed had had difficulties settling into family placements and had only ended a succession of placement moves when they were placed in foster care with a single woman.

These findings suggest that, in exploring placements for children, social workers need to be attentive to the motives of potential male carers, and aware that male children in the same placement could also pose a potential threat. The particular vulnerability of children who have previous experience of sexual abuse may require their foster carer(s) to have relevant training and to be especially carefully assessed.

Physical abuse in foster care

The face to face interviews revealed cases of physical abuse while in foster care. Henry and Marie (brother and sister) had first come into care at the ages of ten and six respectively. Their first foster placement had lasted for a year and they were physically abused throughout.

> As Henry described the abuse during interview he concluded: 'It was like a stereotype of what they (foster parents) were, 'cause you know you watch it on tele and that and they're all horrible. That's what we thought fostering was when we went there.'

Information from the CIC Line indicated that physical abuse from carers was more of a problem for children in foster than residential care, particularly for girls. Reports from children indicated that in 13 of the 20 cases of physical abuse, children were being abused by foster fathers, although a quarter (five children) were abused by both foster carers. (A parent and an unknown person were the abusers of the other two children.)

Children commonly described the physical abuse taking place when their foster mother was out, at work in the evening or socialising. Another group described foster fathers who drank regularly and were more likely to hit them when drunk. Some girls said the abuse started when they became involved in relationships with boys. Others described foster parents who used physical abuse as a form of discipline.

Six of the 20 children reporting physical abuse had been similarly abused in the past and half of these were in care as a result of physical abuse. Children who had come into care because of physical abuse were particularly affronted to find they were being abused again in foster care.

Children were often very upset and scared to talk about the physical abuse they were suffering. Some had told adults about their problems but had not been believed, or the adult had felt they were exaggerating. One child showed her social worker the bruises inflicted by her foster father; the latter, she said, simply replied, "He must have done it for a reason."

Part of the family

Adapting to different family values and life styles was hard for some children in foster care. Occasionally children were placed in a home which was so incompatible with their previous life experiences as to challenge their identity.

> Sabah, a Muslim child, had been placed in a Hindu foster family. Although it was only a temporary placement, Sabah felt very uncomfortable and was angry that the social worker had known her religion, and yet had still placed her with this family.

Generally, children called about less fundamental aspects of their foster placement. They described how they felt restricted by the values of the foster family; others didn't like the food they prepared or were confused about some of the rules the family wanted them to adopt. Most of these children were unsure of where the boundaries were in relation to the foster parents and did not feel confident enough to challenge their decisions or rules. Several said during interview and in calls to the CIC Line that they felt they had to be careful not to overstep the mark for fear of losing the placement. Clearly this tension around their position, and insecurity about the future, meant that for some children the experience of foster care was very artificial. These issues were more likely to be raised by older children, presumably more established in their values than younger children.

Some felt the root of their problems in the foster home lay in being fostered by people who were only interested in the money received for looking after them. Another explanation children gave was that, as foster children, the family viewed them as dispensable and easily replaced; if they did not fit in they would have to leave.

> As Mark, a 12-year-old in foster care, said to a counsellor on the CIC Line:
> "Foster carers are OK but they send you back if they don't want you".

Children placed with foster parents who had no children of their own were generally more confident about their position, although there was some indication that occasionally childless foster carers had unreasonable expectations of the children. For example, problems with boyfriends or other common issues seemed to be attributed to their status as fostered children.

Young people reported that the relationships with other children within the foster home could be both a source of support and frustration. Generally children found the presence of other foster children in the placement very positive. They provided an opportunity to share their experiences with someone who would be able to empathise with them and children had developed strong friendships with other foster children in the same placement.

Foster carers' own children were more likely to be a source of conflict, usually as a result of the foster carers' behaving differently towards the foster child. Children described placements where the foster parents seemed openly to favour their own children above the foster child or children. Some gave material examples of this favouritism. Others talked about how they felt foster carers extended this to discipline and other matters, generally adopting a more lenient or loving approach to their own children.

Interviewers observed material evidence of foster carers favouring their own children. It was not uncommon to find foster children squeezed into a shabby box room while the carers' own child enjoyed a more luxurious or spacious bedroom. The policy on children's photographs in the foster home was often a good indication of attitudes. Some foster carers gave their own children exclusive rights to the wall or mantel space for displaying family photographs. Others were, however, more sensitive to the foster child's needs for recognition, too.

Children who felt most isolated were those who were in longer term foster placements but who had no sense of belonging to the foster family. Many of these children experienced life as second-class citizens, there 'on trial'. In these cases, the children found the tension between the physical proximity of the family, and yet being kept at an emotional distance, understandably very difficult to cope with. Some children who had previously been in residential care also felt isolated in their foster placements. As Shireen (16) explained during interview:

> "It's very difficult after you've been living in a children's home for a long time to go into a family, 'cause you can't relate"

Interviews indicated that children who were in short-term foster care to alleviate family tensions generally had lower expectations of the placement. They were usually young people who had a particular difficulty with one or both of their natural parents. These were some of the most satisfied children, who had come to realise the value of a short separation. Most had no expectation that they would become part of the foster family. They regarded the placement as temporary accommodation which helped to relieve tensions in their own family.

Summary of foster care findings

The foster children who felt most comfortable in their foster placements were those who were in long-term placements and encouraged to be part of the family. These children felt secure enough to have a say in how they lived their life. They were confident that they were cared for and generally regarded their foster parents as surrogate parents. Similarly, children who were in planned short-term placements (and were fully aware of their temporary status) were usually comfortable with the notion that they were in foster care to alleviate some transient problem in their family circumstances. Their expectations of the placement were lower.

Children who are unhappy with their foster placements may be experiencing the effects of separation but it is clear that this is exacerbated by a foster family which maintains inflexible rules or simply views the child as a source of income. When foster carers favour their own children in terms of space, material goods and most importantly, in love and affection, this is particularly painful for children separated from their own family, who are looking for a home they can call their own.

Children who were experiencing abuse in foster care generally felt extremely isolated and confused. For those children who had been taken into care as a result of similar abuse, the experience was doubly horrifying. In the case of abusive foster fathers there was every indication that the abuse was planned and in some cases this included exploitation of the knowledge that children had been abused before. The abuse of young women by older male children of the foster carers was also disturbing. It suggests the need when social workers are seeking foster placements, to be attentive to the age and gender differences between foster children and carers' own children, to prepare foster families, including their own children, thoroughly for the arrival of the foster children, and to support foster children through visits.

Seeking help with problems

Children interviewed face to face were specifically asked what they did when they had a problem, who they felt they could talk to about everyday and more serious issues, and what type of help and support they had from staff or foster carers, social workers, family and friends. Children counselled on the CIC Line also discussed others with whom they had shared their problems. Many were encouraged by ChildLine counsellors to identify someone, in their immediate network, with whom they could talk their problems through. The information presented below summarises the views given by children about how they tackle their problems and who can and does help them resolve these.

Running away

Forty (7%) of the children calling the CIC Line had run away to escape a problem they were experiencing in care. The proportion who had run away from foster families was roughly the same as the proportion who had run away from residential homes.

Runaways included both children who had just entered care and those who had been in the care system for years. They identified a wide variety of problems which they felt had caused them to run, but most had not taken the decision to do so lightly. These children described having discussed their problems with others before running away and thinking through alternatives before finally making the decision to run. Some had run away in the past and a few described themselves as constantly running away and returning, but in most cases they had planned to run away because they felt they had no alternative at the time.

Thirty-five per cent of the children who had run away (14) were being bullied or experiencing some form of abuse - sexual, physical or emotional - in their placement. The others had a variety of problems including dissatisfaction with their placement or carer(s). These children were likely to be feeling very frightened or frustrated with their inability to resolve their problems. They reported that they had either run away to escape their problem - " I've just had enough, I can't take no more" - or to highlight how strongly they felt to carers or professionals engaged in making decisions on their behalf.

Children were most likely to run away to a friend or relative. A few had run away with no place in mind and had ended up living rough in disused buildings or in a park. Interestingly, most of the children felt they would, inevitably, return to care at some point, when their money ran out or they could no longer stay with a friend. But they hoped that the act of running away would precipitate a change in their circumstances on their return.

Managing feelings

Stewart had been taken into care as a result of violently attacking his stepfather, who Stewart said had repeatedly beaten him and his mother. In care, Stewart had found that at certain points his emotions became unmanageable and he started to feel very aggressive. He described the process:

> "It all depends how I get out of bed. If I feel all right in the morning if I think about it (abuse by stepfather) it doesn't bother me. If I get out in a stroppy mood I think about it and I get stressed out an unbelievable amount."

> Stewart had taken to playing football as a way of managing these feelings. He discussed how he had been involved in some 'near miss' fights with friends at the football club and other residents in the home. Stewart felt that in some of these fights he was so out of control that he could have seriously hurt someone. Stewart had yet to receive advice and support in exploring and dealing with these feelings.

Around a third of the children interviewed face to face and calling the CIC Line described the kind of emotional difficulties experienced by Stewart, although they took different forms for different children. For some, these periods of emotional turmoil were resolved in bouts of depression, others inflicted wounds on themselves, felt suicidal or tried to isolate themselves until they felt better. Much more common among boys were periods of aggression where they continually fought with others, both verbally and physically. Girls were more likely to act out violent feelings on inanimate objects, as in the case of Lynette who described how she would go into her bedroom, turn her mattress up against the wall and 'kick hell out of it' until she felt better. Others said they simply 'played up' for a while or 'behaved badly' when they were experiencing these feelings.

For all these children, the strain of containing and managing their feelings was apparent at various points. Most of them were not sure why they had such feelings but all were well aware of their own patterns of behaviour. Fundamentally, the children felt that these phases of emotional chaos were an inescapable dimension of their lives and that they had to cope with them alone.

Who children tell

During interviews children described how they would talk through their problems and worries with someone else. From their accounts it became apparent that a number of factors influenced who children approached with specific problems, notably the age of the child, the number of previous placements they had had and the type of problem they were experiencing.

Generally, the younger the child, the more likely they were to talk to an adult carer about their problems. Children under 14, who were settled in the foster placement, generally felt they could take their problems to one or both of their foster carers, usually the foster mother. Even when they knew they had a problem which could only be resolved by their social worker, they preferred to communicate through the foster carer. Similarly, younger children in residential care were more likely to approach their key worker or a member of staff in the home.

With older children, the nature of the problem seemed to be very influential in decisions about whom to approach. Generally the more personal and difficult a problem, the less likely they were to take it to a carer or social worker, or indeed any adult. In these situations, friends tended to be the main confidant. For example, 36 per cent of the children calling the CIC Line with a pregnancy problem had only discussed it with a friend. They were also most likely to share other complex problems such as abuse, relationship or sexual issues, with a friend.

The friends they approached were generally outside the current placement. Although there were cases of children developing close friendships with another resident or foster child of the same placement, more usually friendships had been made while living at home and had been maintained since. Children described their friends as easy to approach and more willing to listen than most of the adults in their lives.

> Angela (16) had been taken into care at the age of ten because of family problems. She had experienced a series of placement changes. Starting off in foster care, she was eventually placed in what she described as a 'dreadful' children's home which had since been closed. On arrival at the home, Angela was shocked at the level of violence between residents "..the lasses there were really hard, they kicked the hell out of ye and the lads would as well." Angela tried to lock herself in her room but that did not stop the attacks. After six months she ran away. She cycled all day to reach the house of her old school friend, Claire, whom she had met when she was eight years old. She stayed

with Claire's family for a while, who later called her social worker and demanded a change of placement.

Angela was moved to another children's home, of which she said, "I was pleased about the move but I didn't like the way some of the male staff treated the kids". She described male workers who gave children uninvited hugs and kisses and the same workers slapping children round the head when they behaved badly. Angela was also disturbed when staff failed to intervene when the residents were physically fighting. "They'd just say, 'Let them get on with it, they'll sort themselves out,' but I used to say, 'Yes, but it's not right,' 'cause I'd had enough of seeing violence and stuff."

Fortunately, Angela was able to get through these experiences with the support of her 'best mate', Claire, who lived close to the second home and whom she saw regularly. Angela lived in the second residential home for several years. When she was 14 she felt she needed more independence than the children's home offered. She repeatedly asked to be moved to a more independent environment. Angela said, "They (staff and social worker) wouldn't listen to me. I told them and they wouldn't listen." One evening Angela felt so desperate that she took a mixture of over 70 tablets in a suicide attempt. Fortunately, Angela called her friend Claire 'to say goodbye'. Claire immediately knew that something was wrong, arranged for an ambulance to be called to the home and alerted staff. Angela spent a week in hospital and was moved to a semi-independent living unit soon afterwards.

Older children were more likely to tell residential staff and foster carers about problems associated with their placement, particularly violence and bullying by other children in residential homes, and concerns about food and living conditions.

Children found it particularly difficult to talk about sexual abuse. Of all those calling the CIC Line with a problem related to past or present abuse (which had sometimes led to their running away) nearly a third (22 children) had been unable to speak to anyone about their experiences.

The case of Cassy illustrates one of the reasons why children may be reluctant to confide more personal problems in their carers:

Cassy was taken into care at the age of six because her mother couldn't cope. She described the problems she had with a foster carer at the age of ten. "They used to try and make me talk about my Dad and I really didn't know him. I says to them, 'Look, I don't want to talk about him,' and it used to drive me mad, I used to lose my temper really bad. They were trying to force me to talk about things I didn't want to talk about. I told them and I just flipped out and lashed out in the end. I'd had enough."

Children who described experiences like Cassy's felt carers had been insensitive to their feelings and their needs at the time. Many gave examples which demonstrated carers lacking the skills to talk and listen to children.

Several of the children in residential care also identified the difficulty of finding an opportunity to talk privately to a member of staff; they said they were always too busy or had a more pressing matter on hand. Others reported incidents where they had talked to staff, only to find their conversation had been relayed to other staff in the home.

The absence of confidentiality was also a reason given for not speaking to other residents in a children's home. As Michael, a 12-year-old in residential care put it during interview:

> "No, don't trust 'em, you tell 'em something and they just go and blab it off. You just learn not to say anything to 'em."

The situation for children in foster care was similar. Apart from the younger children described earlier and those relatively unusual cases where children were well established in long-term placements, children described a reluctance to talk to foster carers about more personal matters. For some this was an attempt to maintain a placement, where they felt talking about certain areas to their foster carers would cause friction and undermine their position. Typical 'no go' conversation areas were sex, sexuality, depression, relationships with natural parents and personal relationships.

Children who knew they would be returning home, or who were determined to do so, felt they had to maintain an emotional distance from their carers. Others felt it was inappropriate to discuss very personal matters with carers who were at that stage almost strangers to them.

Social workers were described as the most distant figures for children. They were usually approached by children for support in dealing with some problem related to their placement, often after the matter had already been discussed with a carer. Although social workers generally knew about children's life histories and were thus privy to the experiences which were likely to raise problems for them in the future, children rarely felt close enough to their social worker to discuss personal problems. Children in foster care were the most distant from their social workers in this respect, many feeling they had no means of contacting the social worker other than through their carers. Consequently, social workers were generally only called upon to deal with practical matters, such as payments and arrangements to visit relatives.

In those rare cases where social workers had taken (or been given) the time to get to know the child, and regularly spoke to the child alone, children found them a valuable source of support. As Jill, a 16-year-old in residential care said of a social worker she had had in the past:

> "She was really good. She gave you good advice and I felt like there was someone on my side that was willing to help me and, you know, show me the right directions."

Another significant factor deterring children from approaching the adults in their lives seemed to be the number of previous placements they had had. Children who had experienced over three placement breakdowns were less likely to trust the adults currently in their lives. These children felt let down by previous carers, and were reluctant to invest time and energy in developing new relationships. The same was true of children who had developed close relationships with past carers or residents, who had later moved away from the placement.

Summary

These findings indicate that, apart from younger children and those who had established a secure placement, children in public care were most likely to turn to friends for emotional support in dealing with very personal problems and situations they perceived as serious. Generally for those children who grew up in care and experienced several placement breakdowns, the likelihood of their turning to a carer or social worker for help and advice became more remote. Their experiences led them to believe that friends were likely to provide a more enduring and confidential source of support. Other children found that telling others had not helped them resolve their problems. Some experienced difficulties that they were unable to express verbally. These children described running away, emotional outbursts and acts of self-destruction as means of communicating the pain they were experiencing.

The findings revealed that although a few children do run away on the spur of the moment, these are likely to return fairly quickly. The determined runaways had more deliberate intentions, and were likely to be experiencing a specific problem in their placement which they felt unable to express or resolve. Many felt unloved or not listened to and had explored a number of alternatives before deciding to run. They were likely to run away to a friend or relative and stay away longer. Most runaways are looking for a change in their placement or a response to their concerns. The fact that some repeatedly run away is testimony to the fact that the problem persists on their return.

Other sources of support

Family contacts

Children who called the CIC Line revealed that they often maintained contact with one or more relatives. In most cases (28%) this was their mother. Children also kept in contact with siblings (25%). Interviews suggested that although these family contacts were very important to children, their visits to meet relatives were often very strained. Children who were in care because of family relationship problems were generally aware that their return home was to some extent dependent on their visits being harmonious and positive. As Michael's experiences demonstrate, this was not always the case.

> Michael was in residential care to ease relations between himself and his mother. She found him unmanageable and they had argued constantly when living together. In an attempt to return home quickly, Michael had visited his mother regularly and been on his best behaviour. Michael was returned home quickly only to find that the arguments continued. He concluded that "Me and me Mum get on better when we're not living together, we just can't get along."

Children who wanted to return home were very keen to maintain regular contact with their family and relatives. But in some cases their families were reluctant to visit children or only visited intermittently. These children generally felt confused by their parents' behaviour and over time this had led some to feel ambivalent about returning home.

Children who had no sense that they would return home or who did not want to do so, (usually children who had been abused) expressed mixed feelings about maintaining family contacts. These children were more likely to maintain contact with a more distant relative, for instance, a grandmother. Contact with their parent(s), particularly abusive parents, was so limited and controlled that children found it hard to cope with.

Some younger children wanted to maintain contact with an abusive parent but had not been allowed to do so.

Siblings

Relationships with siblings seemed less prone to confusion. Children were enthusiastic about maintaining contact with brothers and sisters and, where they had been able to do so, this was likely to provide positive support.

> Michelle, a 15-year-old girl in residential care, described how she was taken into care at the age of 14. Before that time she had lived with her older sister and had wanted to stay with her but had been unable to do so. She went to stay with her sister regularly and they spoke on the 'phone. Michelle's sister had recently been encouraging her to go to college when she left school. Michelle said: "She's been giving me positive input and telling me to do something with myself and be somebody. I think that's really helped me to see what I want out of life."

Despite the strong research evidence to suggest that, where possible, siblings in care should be kept together, *(Berridge & Cleaver 1987; Dolphin Project, 1993)* a number of children had been separated from their siblings. Separation was more common among families with more than two children placed in foster care; presumably because of the difficulties of placing more than this number in a single foster placement. Children calling the CIC Line and those interviewed found the process of separation from their siblings one of the most painful aspects of coming into public care. Children (particularly from abusive families) had developed close supportive relationships with their siblings. Other children were uneasy about the fact that they were the only child in care when siblings remained at home.

A small group of children appear to have experienced particularly clumsy social work practice in relation to their siblings. There were some instances where children had been promised that they would be reunited with a sibling but this had not happened. Other cases demonstrated the difficulties of siblings having different social workers. One child had experienced a foster home breakdown and was moved into a residential home on an emergency basis. She was 'over the moon' to find that one of her younger brothers was in the same home, only to find that he was moved without explanation two days later. Another believed she had discovered a long-lost brother at her new school, but it took social workers two months to confirm this formally.

ChildLine

During face to face interviews, children were asked what they thought of ChildLine and the CIC Line in particular. All the children interviewed knew of the existence of ChildLine's main 0800 1111 service, but had different ideas about the type of problems dealt with by ChildLine. Older children tended to believe that ChildLine was a crisis helpline, mainly for children who had been abused, while younger children were more likely to know that they could take any problem to ChildLine. Although some of the older children, notably boys, felt that they were unlikely to use ChildLine, they were unanimous in the belief that it provided a valuable service.

Others described having called ChildLine in the past. Most felt ChildLine had helped them both to understand their problem and to decide what to do about it. A significant complaint from children who had called the main 0800 1111 number was that it was hard to get through to a counsellor.

Children's knowledge of the special CIC Line was more limited. Most had not heard of it, while others thought it had closed. Children living with foster families generally had less information about the Line than those in residential homes, possibly because of the relative difficulty of getting information to individual children in foster care. Those who did know about the CIC Line were clear that it was designed to help children like themselves and knew that they would have a better chance of getting through to a counsellor on this line than on the main number.

Overall, children particularly valued the confidential nature of the ChildLine service and the fact that it could be used anonymously. Some children felt the service would be especially useful to children who had no one else to talk to.

Making private telephone calls

Users of the CIC Line reported various difficulties in finding a 'phone they could use in private. Thirteen per cent were interrupted by carers and other children, while being counselled by ChildLine. In some cases, staff asked children to stop using the telephone or to hurry up. Children were more likely to tease the child who was telephoning ChildLine.

The face to face interviews with children revealed that telephones in residential homes were unlikely to be situated in a private area; most were in corridors or close to the staff office. In smaller homes, children were usually allowed to use the staff telephone for private calls but sometimes had to ask the staff first. Use of the telephone was also sometimes restricted to certain times of the day.

It was evident that making a telephone call in private was harder for younger children, as they generally had less freedom to leave their placements unsupervised. Although some of these children suggested they could use a public telephone at school or on their journey to and from school, public telephones were not without their own difficulties. Children calling the CIC Line from a public 'phone box would on occasions feel obliged to end their call because others were waiting to use the 'phone.

Summary

Most of the children calling the CIC Line and those interviewed face to face had some contact with a member of their family. This was often their mother or another female relative. These contacts were not without difficulties. In maintaining contact with their families, children experienced a range of problems, many to do with whether or not they expected to return home. Contacts with siblings were less prone to confusion.

Children were unanimously supportive of the services provided by ChildLine, even when they felt they were unlikely to use them. Those who had used the main ChildLine service were likely to have experienced difficulties getting through to a counsellor. The use of ChildLine's services is dependent on children having free access to a telephone they can use in privacy. The findings suggest that for some children, notably younger children and those in residential care, access to telephones is restricted in various ways.

Education and plans for the future

Research suggests that children being looked after can lose out educationally, particularly through the disruption of leaving home and when they experience repeated placement changes within the care system *(Jackson, 1989; Audit Commission, 1994).* Of the children calling the CIC Line who gave information about their placement, 39 per cent had only been in one placement and very few had needed to move schools when they went into care. Only five rang with a problem about school.

Of the children who called the CIC Line, those who had experienced three or more placements were more likely to have moved schools. The face to face interviews gave more insight into the impact of these changes. It was clear that children often found it traumatic to move school while they were in care. Children recalled being very concerned not to tell people at school that they were in care, in case this led to bullying or being rejected by the other children. Some maintained a complex web of deceit to disguise their looked after status. Others simply referred to their carers as 'Mum and Dad' to ease communication with children at school. Residential care seemed more difficult in this context than foster care - children described simply avoiding the issue of parents until they felt confident enough to tell a few selected individuals. Children were also generally unsure about whether their teachers knew they were being looked after. As one ten-year-old in foster care put it:

> "They (teachers) do, 'cause like on the dinner money cheques, we have cheques. Lou (foster mother) puts her signature on the bottom of the cheque and on the back she puts my name or otherwise they won't know who's it is and like we've got different names so they know, don't they."

Whatever the strategy employed, children clearly had problems being open about the fact that they were in care. For some, past experience of being teased or 'picked on' because they were in local authority care was the basis of this fear. Others simply felt ashamed or feared being rejected by the other children. For a small minority the strain of school was such that they had 'got into trouble' for fighting with other children. A few had resorted to truancy.

Even when children had not changed schools, they had uneasy feelings about going back to school from their placement in care. Most were still confused and upset about having come into care and felt detached from the people and activities in school. Some had been helped through this stage by other children at the school who were also in the care system

Another problem particularly evident in residential placements was the lack of privacy and space in which to study. As Danielle (17) described it during interview:

> "When I was trying to do GCSE's and that and go for my exams. I wasn't able to 'cause everyone used to sleep (go to bed) about 4 or 5 o'clock in the morning. Everyone was upstairs running up and down, banging on my door, asking for cigarettes, asking me for this, asking me for that or if they could come down and sit down. All I wanted was a bit of peace and quiet, you know, and I didn't get none of that and I always complained about that."

In view of these findings, it was surprising that most of the children interviewed were still keen to achieve at school. Their aspirations for future employment were usually very specific. Commonly children wanted to join the armed forces or pursue a leisure interest on a professional basis.

In contrast to their clear ideas for future employment, children were more unsure about their future living circumstances. The only children who felt clear about where they would be living after leaving care were those on the verge of leaving, or those in stable foster placements, who had been promised a home 'for as long as they needed it'. This uncertainty about the future was indicative of a general pattern where longer-term planning had a very low profile. Generally children interviewed were aware of the short-term plans for their future but these were unlikely to extend beyond the following six to 12 months. Interestingly, in the absence of any clear indication from carers and social workers about their long-term futures, children generally concluded that they would either return home or rent a bedsit.

Commonly children in residential care felt they would immediately return home when they left care. Some viewed the in care experience almost as a prison sentence. Others feared the responsibility of leaving care and felt that it would be difficult to adjust to living alone. Children aged 16 upwards were generally more concerned about the issue of leaving care, presumably because it was a more imminent reality.

These findings suggest that most carers and social workers are preoccupied with the more immediate future. They appear to be planning on a six-monthly cycle with little or no regard for the impact of this on a child's sense of security. It is not surprising in this context that children devise their own plans for the future and feel, like Joanne, a 16-year-old on the verge of leaving care, when she said, "Being in care is about learning to be an adult before your time."

Summary

Returning to school after entering care and changing schools as a result of separation from families can be additional sources of stress for children. Furthermore, children in residential homes may experience particular difficulties in securing time and space to study. Nevertheless, most of the children interviewed still expected to achieve at school and to get jobs as a result.

Children were less sure about their future living arrangements. Long-term plans for children seemed to be rarely available to children or discussed with them.

Conclusions

The Children Act (1989) embraced the notion that 'the child's ascertainable wishes and feelings' are an important consideration in making decisions about children's welfare in public and family law proceedings - *(Children Act, 1989, Part I)*. The idea of working in 'partnership' is a central theme of the Guidance and Regulations issued under the Act.

ChildLine's research has highlighted a number of areas where children continue to feel unsupported and isolated by the care system in England and Wales. It has also identified opportunities for local authorities to increase their partnership arrangements with individual children and with other organisations seeking to support children in need. Fundamentally, children complain of not being heard by the adults in their lives.

Evidence from the Children in Care Line suggests that children have valued the opportunity to discuss, in confidence with an independent person, problems associated with being in care and also more general problems. Some specific areas where children continue to experience difficulty are outlined below.

Coming into care is clearly a traumatic process which leaves children with powerful feelings of loss. There is little indication from this research that the care system addresses these feelings alongside the child. From children's accounts, the process of entering care is characterised by a lack of information, notably on why children are being taken into public care. This gap remains with children and can be exacerbated by the fact that few have subsequently had the opportunity to reassess their experiences or to check their understanding of the reasons for their removal from home. The consistent exceptions to this finding are children who have been abused. They are generally quite clear about why they are in the care system, but many have unresolved feelings about the experiences which have so dramatically affected their lives - notably in how they relate to others and perceive themselves.

The fact that some children report that they are sexually or physically abused by carers or other young people who live with them is extremely disturbing. The findings suggest that children in foster care may be more likely to be targets of abuse - both sexual and physical - particularly if they have previous experiences of abuse. The research also indicates that many of these cases might have been avoided by more careful consideration of placements and increased opportunities for children to express their concerns and wishes. Some children had told adults, including social workers, about their abuse but had not been believed or listened to.

Children in residential care describe a variety of problems with their placements and living environment. Many feel powerless to negotiate alternative arrangements and unsuccessful attempts to do so can leave them feeling angry and frustrated. Bullying seems to be a problem which staff and carers in residential homes have particular difficulty in addressing.

Some children described a situation in which it was left to them to maintain family contacts, establish a life in their placement, deal with emotional problems, prepare for leaving care and formulate a future to which they could look forward. Many of the children included in the research had come to believe that the responsibility for these matters was largely their's. Support from individual carers or social workers was felt to be dependent on the strength of relationship they had been able to establish with them. Any initiative on the part of carers, and so on, was seen to be influenced more by individual personality or motivation than by notions of agreed and acceptable standards of child-care practice.

In the absence of strong family links and particularly for those children who have found themselves 'drifting' in the care system, friends can assume a significant and supportive role. But many of the children using the CIC Line had accumulated a series of problems both before entering care and while in care. The complexity of their problems and the emotions they experience as a result are unlikely to be fully resolved solely by friendships with peers.

A number of factors appear to be inhibiting children from forming supportive relationships within the public care system. Notably, children who have been abused are likely to experience difficulties in relating to others generally. The information available to the children may influence their relations with others, particularly their families. Opportunities to talk in confidence to carers and social workers may be limited or non-existent. Children who have experienced several placement changes may become reluctant to form new relationships.

In the absence of any forum for expressing their problems and concerns children may develop behavioural problems or have sudden emotional outbursts. Others will run away or try to harm themselves. From children's accounts, it appears that the adult response to these manifestations is often a process of containment rather than of exploration.

ChildLine has learnt that children's attempts to talk to adults can often fail because adults do not or cannot respond in ways that the child can use. Children's use of the ChildLine service has revealed that:

- Children may make several attempts to communicate with adults about their problems before they find the courage to speak. This is particularly the case for children who have experienced abuse.

- Children may present their concerns in various ways, for instance, jokey, screaming, as a third party, in the form of a minor problem or using abusive language. These presentations may often break conventional adult expectations of communication about problems.

- Children value the anonymity offered by the telephone and will use this opportunity to test adult reactions and their own ability to speak about their problems. Anonymity can also allow children to feel in control of overwhelming emotions.

- Children are unlikely to respond to an adult who adopts a disbelieving approach or cross-questions them about facts. Particularly in cases of abuse, children may confuse the facts of their story or be genuinely confused by their experiences.

- Children find it helpful when an adult actively listens to their concerns and allows them to describe their feelings in their own terms.

- Fundamentally children respond to being given the space to express their problems in their own language and at their own pace. The discussion should in effect be child-led.

- Listening to children on their own terms may require the adults to check the meaning of what children are saying. Children respond to encouraging, open-ended responses such as, "Can you tell me a bit more about that, I am not sure what you mean," rather than to attempts to reinterpret the child's words in adult terms.

- Some of the problems children present may seem trivial to adults. Nevertheless, even apparently small problems can cause considerable distress to a child.

Children in public care are by definition one of the most vulnerable groups of children in society. Though some children do cope with experiences of loss, abuse and disruption with remarkable resilience and fortitude, ChildLine's research has shown that many feel isolated in the care system and unable to influence their lives, and most have unresolved feelings about coming into care. The provision of additional sources of support can do much to alleviate these problems. The volume, range and depth of calls received on the Children in Care Line demonstrates the need for such support and the value children place on it when it is provided.

Summary and recommendations for local authorities

Introduction

The past few years have seen considerable progress in establishing principles of good practice, complaints procedures and clear guidance to local authorities in England and Wales *(Department of Health, 1989)*. ChildLine's research demonstrates that too large a gap still remains between the guidance and the practice.

All the recommendations which follow are in keeping with the spirit of the DoH guidance and most are to be found there, although not always spelt out so explicitly.

1. Reception into care

The research demonstrates that children and young people need to be given information appropriate to their age about the reasons why they are being looked after. They also require space and opportunities to explore their feelings about the process of coming into care. These areas might need to be regularly revisited by the child, and his or her understanding explored with a carer.

As part of their case planning and review policies, local authorities should ensure that

(i) Children's need to recall and explore their feelings and understanding of why they are being looked after is specifically acknowledged and built into the review requirement.

(ii) Those responsible for the care of the child are aware of specialist counselling services which could be available to children where appropriate. (Some children would particularly benefit from counselling regarding separation from their own families.)

(iii) Children are given adequate information, (both orally and in writing) about
  (a) their personal history
  (b) their rights within the care system,
  (c) what they might reasonably expect of the particular placement by way of acceptable standards of care, individual and collective behaviour among carers and residents, and
  (d) the means available to them for expressing concerns or making a complaint.

2. Managing problems and feelings

The research highlights a number of problems and stresses which children looked after by local authorities are attempting to cope with, notably, previous and current abuse, maintaining links with their family, and relationships with carers and peers and at school. Children may develop sophisticated defence mechanisms to manage their feelings; for some, these prove ineffective or periodically break down, and may result (for example) in bouts of anger, depression, running away, or withdrawal.

Local authorities should consider what additional measures or facilities, by way of training, advice or support, would be helpful to often over-pressed carers in recognising and responding to emotional problems likely to be experienced by young people in local authority care. Specifically, local authorities should ensure that at review each child's need for additional emotional support is considered. The need for carers to receive training in basic counselling work with children, and the value of independent advice or facilities for both carers and children, should also form part of this consideration.

3. Child protection

The research findings supported existing evidence which suggests that children with previous experiences of sexual or physical abuse may be particularly vulnerable to further abuse *(Fromuth 1986, Finkelhor & Browne 1986, Beitchman et al, 1992)*. Many children with abusive experiences described persistent difficulties in relating to others and require special support or counselling if they are to come to terms with their experiences.

i) In the complex process of assessing the suitability of placements for children, those responsible for placement policies and social workers themselves should be especially mindful of the potentially greater vulnerability of abused children, in foster care and residential placements. Particular consideration should be given to the potential threat posed by the presence of older male children living in the placement and male carers (including informal male carers who may have no specific responsibility for working with or caring for the child).

ii) Carers of abused children require particular skills and insights regarding the vulnerability and needs of abused children. The National Foster Care Association has recommended that foster carers' skills should be recognised in the form of a 'payment for skills' policy. ChildLine supports this approach as a practical way of addressing the specific needs of abused children in foster placements.

Children in residential placements indicate particular difficulty in discussing their experiences of past abuse.

Those responsible for children should take a pro-active role in:
(a) providing opportunities for children to identify for themselves a particular worker to whom they feel able to relate and
(b) involving the informal support systems identified by children in the research as helpful; for example, other young people who are, or have been looked after by local authorities, particularly as a result of sexual abuse.

4. Bullying in residential homes

The research findings suggested that bullying is a persistent feature of residential establishments.

i) Local authorities should consider addressing the prevalent problem of bullying by

    (a)   establishing and implementing comprehensive anti-bullying strategies in their homes

    (b)   offering training to staff in managing incidents of bullying, and creating an environment where bullying becomes unacceptable.

ii)   Children who have been bullied may require additional counselling support in dealing with the trauma of these experiences.

5. Education

Children report difficulties in school arising from being in local authority care. The research findings reveal that staff and other children may stigmatise children in public care; or simply may not openly acknowledge and accept the child's looked after status.

i)   Social services departments should endeavour to share with education departments the insights gained from children about their sensitivities regarding their looked after status, and consider appropriate ways of acknowledging this with the child.

ii)   Carers should be encouraged to establish strong links with the schools attended by the children they are caring for.

Children in residential care often report difficulties in gaining the support of carers in pursuing further education. In particular, practical problems to do with lack of space and privacy may affect the child's ability to study in the placement.

iii)   Clearly, all children need access to private and quiet space for various reasons, not least educational. When planning residential provision, attention should be paid by local authorities to the need for such facilities. The development of 'good parenting' policies within homes, which facilitate and encourage educational pursuits, also warrants serious consideration.

iv)   Children should be actively encouraged to explore and pursue education and training through the provision of financial and moral support.

6. Placement considerations

"Measures which antagonise, alienate, undermine or marginalise parents are counter-productive." *(Department of Health, 1989, The care of children)* ChildLine's research showed that children experience considerable difficulties in adapting to the lifestyles of foster parents which are in sharp contrast to those of their own families.

i) When placing children in foster homes, local authorities should strive to ensure that current guidance on social class and cultural aspects of children's lives is given due attention, to ensure that placements do not undermine or marginalise children's own families.

Children (particularly older children) who have lived in residential homes for some time report difficulties in adapting to the more intimate family environment of a foster placement.

ii) For children with a relatively long residential care history there would be merit in considering placements where the family structure is flexible and less intimate. The existence of other foster children within the foster home appears helpful in these circumstances.

Children report that difficulties sometimes arise when foster parents' own children are still living at home.

iii) There would be value in always exploring with prospective and existing foster carers how they will manage the relationships, and potentially competing interests, between their own children and any foster children sharing the home.

iv) Working with foster carers' children to prepare them for the arrival of foster siblings would also be helpful.

Children being looked after by local authorities are often critical of decision-making processes, notably in relation to placements and aspects of their living environment. They describe feeling unheard, intimidated or marginalised in decisions about their lives.

v) The importance of social workers, carers and others with decision-making responsibility communicating with children and listening to what they have to say cannot be over-estimated. Training in communication and active listening skills should be a priority for all who work closely with children.

vi) Local authorities should also consider as a matter of policy using independent advocates to help children to present their views when important decisions about their future are being made (particularly in more formal situations such as case conferences).

7. Leaving care

Older children nearing the care-leaving age describe feeling unprepared for leaving care and uncertain about their future living arrangements. This is a further source of stress for children, some of whom have drifted into fantasy and wishful thinking. Others anticipate a life of isolation.
Children leaving care need further support in managing the transition from public care to independent living.

(i) Local authorities should review this aspect of their care-planning process, ensuring that as early as possible and throughout their lives in care, children are involved in immediate short-term and long-term plans for their future and are given information in a way that they can understand.

(ii) Local authorities should consider partnership arrangements with voluntary and youth organisations to provide the following types of support for care leavers:

- semi-independent living arrangements
- individual programmes of preparation for living independently
- links with other young people who have left, or are on the point of leaving care.

Implications of research findings for ChildLine

1. Access to the ChildLine service

Children in care who might otherwise not have thought of telephoning ChildLine or who have been unable to get through to a counsellor on the main 0800 1111 number, have used the alternative free number, 0800 884444, specifically for children in care, to seek advice, guidance and comfort.

i) ChildLine will try to secure the continuing existence of ChildLine for Children in Care in order that this very vulnerable group of children can receive a prompt, on-going response to their need for confidential help and advice.

ii) ChildLine will also continue to work on making the CIC Line more widely known to children in care.

2. Increasing links with face to face counselling and advocacy services

It is clear that looked after children often feel unable to talk with care workers or with other adults who are close to them. In any case, these adults may not be able to address all the needs of children and young people for whom they are responsible.

i) ChildLine will continue to pursue and facilitate the development of advocates, or independent representatives, for children and young people in care.

ii) ChildLine wishes to provide a resource data base to enable children in care to get access to face to face counselling, advice, guidance and support when necessary.

3. Publicity for ChildLine for Children in Care and outreach work

ChildLine is aware from its main 0800 1111 service and from previous research studies that children who cannot read or write or who have special needs because of age or disability may find it difficult to ring ChildLine. Culture, race, religion and sexual identity also appear to have implications for the way that children use the service.

i) ChildLine must give more thought to the most effective ways of publicising, and assisting children to use, its services to children.

ii) As an overall priority, ChildLine will continue actively to seek out and make public the views of children and young people in care about their lives and experiences.

PART TWO

Research findings in Scotland

Research findings in Scotland

Introduction

This section of the report is based on calls received on the Children in Care (CIC) Scotland Line and a number of face to face interviews conducted with children in the Scottish regions.

The caller statistics used in the report are taken from calls to the CIC Scotland Line during the period October 1992 to March 1993, (the first six months of the Line's operation.) The total number of calls answered during this period was 826. The number of children receiving substantial counselling was 137. The calls from the children who were counselled form the basis of the following report, supplemented by 17 face to face interviews with children in care in Scotland. All 17 children agreed to be interviewed and were told in advance the issues to be covered, and the terms on which the interview would be carried out (see Appendices 1-3).

The aim of the interviews was to provide a context for the information from counselling calls and create a broader base of reference for young people's experiences in care. The participating children were in various types of care, including foster families and a range of residential children's homes. They were spread between two regions with differing demographic compositions and care provisions, in both rural and urban areas.

An important point to bear in mind is that the main role of ChilldLine's counsellors is to counsel and not to collect information for research. For this reason, many areas of information useful for purposes of research are not covered in all records. Nevertheless, the report offers a view of the care system from the children within it, thus providing a valuable source of information for future policy-makers and people working in the field of child care.

The number of adults calling the CIC Scotland Line was high in comparison with England and Wales, (14 per cent of total calls compared with three per cent in England and Wales for the same period.) However, as the Line became more established and recognised as a resource primarily for children, the number of adult callers gradually diminished.

Forty-two percent of adult calls related to concerns about children, usually those of relatives or neighbours. These calls were concentrated on issues of neglect and physical or sexual abuse, and the majority of concerns expressed were for female children. Callers were usually seeking advice on the most appropriate action to take.

Analysis of calls to the line

About children calling

Most children calling the CIC Scotland Line were aged between 14 and 16.

Children calling varied greatly in the amount of time they had spent in care and the types of placement they had experienced. The problems which children mentioned did not significantly correlate with specific types of placement.

Most calls were received between 6.30 and 9 p.m. Nine p.m. appears to be the 'cut off' time for calls from children's homes.

Where callers named the region where they lived, 51 per cent were from Strathclyde. This undoubtedly reflects the concentration of population in that region. None of the calls answered were identified as coming from the least populated areas (Highlands, Borders, Western Isles, Shetland and Orkney). There could be a number of reasons for this. ChildLine's past experience suggests that one of the most likely is anxiety about confidentiality. In sparsely populated areas, children in care might not wish to mention where they are calling from, for fear of being identified.

The greatest differences between the national population of children in care in Scotland and the children who called the CIC Scotland Line were in gender and type of placement. The national Scottish Office figures[1] show that 60 per cent of children in care in Scotland are male; also, many, although in care, still live at home. In contrast, 60 per cent of callers to the CIC Scotland Line were female and of those who told us where they lived, 55 per cent were in some sort of residential home – almost the direct opposite of the national situation.

The disproportionately high number of calls from residential placements could be due to a greater awareness of the Line in this setting. Another reason could be that children living at home may not think of themselves as being 'in care' or may not have problems specific to being in care, and therefore did not use the CIC Scotland Line or did not specify their type of placement when calling.

TABLE 1
Scottish national figures 1991 CIC Figures (Oct 92 - Mar 93)

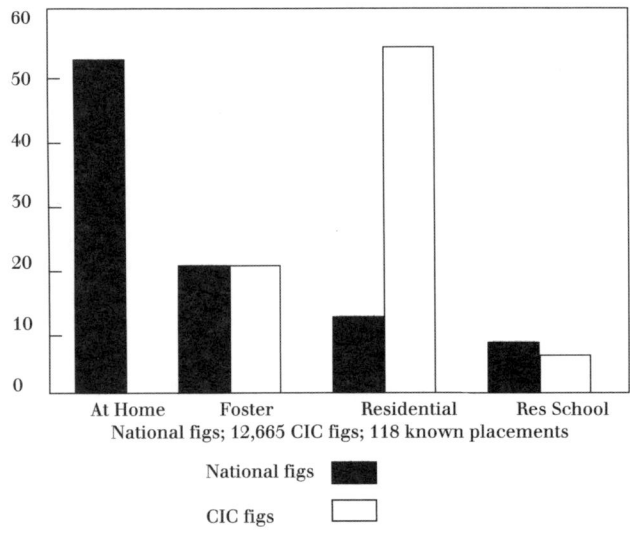

National figs; 12,665 CIC figs; 118 known placements

1 (Source: The Scottish Office Statistical Bulletin *Social work series*, January 1994)

Table 1 shows the comparison between ChildLine and Scottish Office figures. Of the children who told us about their placements, 55 per cent (65) were in children's homes, compared with only ten per cent of children in care in Scotland generally. The 24 children who said they were calling from foster care represent 20 per cent of total calls; this reflects the national figures for children in foster care accurately.

The rest of the callers lived in a variety of placements, including homes with education on site, and semi-independent living units or accommodation.

Children's main problems

When children called the CIC Scotland line, they often began by talking about one specific, or predominant issue which was then coded as their main problem. This was often interlinked with many other issues the children saw as problematic. The following information is divided into the most common main issues about which children telephoned.

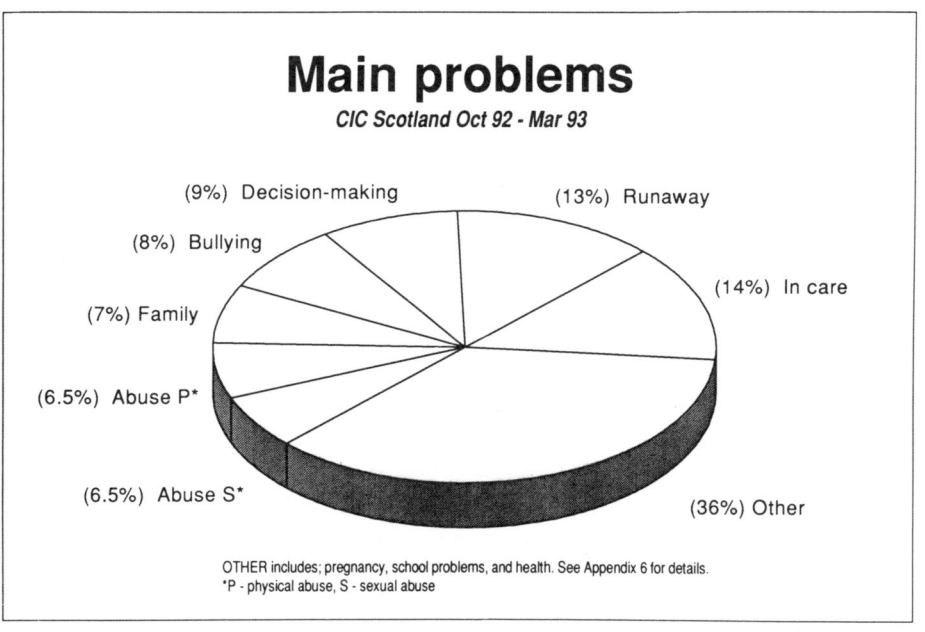

Main problems
CIC Scotland Oct 92 - Mar 93

- (9%) Decision-making
- (8%) Bullying
- (7%) Family
- (6.5%) Abuse P*
- (6.5%) Abuse S*
- (13%) Runaway
- (14%) In care
- (36%) Other

OTHER includes; pregnancy, school problems, and health. See Appendix 6 for details.
*P - physical abuse, S - sexual abuse

Being in care

This was the largest category, accounting for 19 calls (14 per cent of the total). It included children calling about their reception into care, sanctions, living conditions and dissatisfaction with placements.

The findings suggest that the process of reception into care can be extremely daunting. The Children's Hearing system was generally seen as the most positive part of the process, although children felt it could be intimidating. Most children thought the Children's Panel members were attempting to act in their best interests, but that social workers did not always make clear representations to the Panel on their behalf. Children's knowledge and memory of the process of arriving at their present placement was relatively well-informed. Of the total number of children who used the Line, 37 per cent (51 callers) gave a reason why they were in care and knew their legal status.

The issues of concern to children who called about reception into care were often based around day to day living. Many children felt they were restricted by their new situation, often being given a very different set of boundaries to live within. Some of these children felt they had no help or support in settling into this new environment from either social workers or the social work department. Children calling from foster care faced additional problems of settling into a new family structure. In all, 32 per cent of children calling the Line specifically stated they were unhappy with some aspect of their placement or the way they were looked after.

Placement dissatisfactions

Generally, children who were unhappy in their placement but had not yet discussed their concerns with staff had clear ideas on how they would cope. Some were adamant that they wanted to return home, despite a serious risk of abuse in some cases. They felt this would be easier to deal with than coping with the care environment. Others were equally determined to remain in care until they felt ready to leave. Some children expressed concern that they would be expected to begin to live independently as soon as they reached the age of 16. Other children wanted the right to move from placements in which they were unhappy, a request which seemed to be most often denied. Most of the calls received requesting moves from the current placement appeared to be based on quite serious and powerful reasons; for example:

> Jason said he was being bullied by another resident in his children's home. He had told staff who had repeatedly spoken to the perpetrator about his behaviour and taken away some of his privileges, but all to no effect:
>
> Jason had no allocated key worker and felt telling staff had generally made the situation worse. When he called ChildLine he had given up approaching staff, and felt that leaving the home was the only effective solution.

Sanctions

Another contentious issue for children was the imposition of sanctions. Callers gave examples of carers applying blanket rules irrespective of the child's particular needs or circumstances. These included not being prepared to negotiate issues such as bedtimes, reduction of pocket money or withdrawal of activities. Children sometimes felt staff were not responding to them as individuals, and that sanctions were meted out arbitrarily. Some calls were from children who reported being threatened with a move to another unit if they refused to comply with staff requests.

> Lucy told us she did not want to go on weekend leave any more as she did not get on with the community parents with whom she was placed. Lucy had been told that unless she continued to do so she would be moved to a secure unit, since there was no weekend facility at her own unit and this was the only alternative on offer.

Children who mentioned sanctions often said that they were in any case ineffective in curbing unacceptable behaviour. Children said they would prefer to negotiate with staff to solve problems and have other residents included in decisions about how to identify and deal with unacceptable behaviour.

Runaways

Eighteen callers (13 per cent of the total calls) telephoned about running away. Half of these calls were from children placed in children's homes.

The cases in general were scattered throughout the regions, suggesting no particular correlation with differences in child care provisions.

Many of these callers cited restrictions on their actions and no privacy as main reasons for running away (for instance, going to bed early, food at fixed times, shared rooms and, 'staff always on back'). On the surface these may seem trivial; however, placed in context with other information this is not necessarily so. The same callers also told counsellors about their attempts to negotiate with staff or carers which had met with little response. They reported other residents having similar experiences and, in most cases, said that on complaining they were threatened with sanctions or being moved elsewhere, or they simply felt intimidated. The most common comment by far was, "No one listens to what I say/want."

None of the callers in this section knew of an official complaints procedure, and overall, only five of the 137 children who were counselled on the CIC Scotland Line mentioned that they knew of the existence of one.

All the children calling about running away said they felt unable to approach their social worker, or another adult in a position of authority with whom they could negotiate, or who could take action on their behalf. ChildLine counsellors took on this role in several cases, referring children on to appropriate agencies which, in several cases, were in fact their own social work departments.

Decision-making

Calls in this category were from children who were expecting to move to or from a placement or their home against their express wishes. Nine per cent, (13 callers,) are included in this category. The majority of these calls were from children in residential homes. This might be due to increased feelings of insecurity, for example, in short-term placements, when children knew they would be moving on. Poor communication with the social work department, particularly if there was no allocated key worker, could also add to feelings of vulnerability.

Five callers in this group said they were under pressure to return home – mostly from social workers and/or their social work department. Four of the callers had suffered physical abuse in the past; all had experienced a continuation of the abuse while on access visits home, but were too afraid to tell anyone. Other callers feared abuse would begin again if they returned home at that particular point. For example:

> Sam was afraid to return home as he believed his mother would continue to abuse him physically. This was due to the disruptive presence of her boyfriend which had caused tension in the past.

Dissatisfaction with their role in deciding their future was a general problem mentioned by 28 children – one in five of the total who called the CIC Scotland Line. Twenty five (18 per cent) specifically said that they were unhappy with their social worker. Many said this was because their views were not being taken into consideration or listened to when decisions were made about them. Children felt their social workers or their social work departments were only listening to them when it fitted in with departmental plans, and that no real value was placed on views expressed by the children themselves.

Bullying

The majority of children calling about bullying were female, with an average age of 14. Eight out of the eleven callers, for whom bullying was their main problem, were placed in children's homes, and all cited other residents as those responsible. The majority of these callers had approached staff for help and reported an unsatisfactory response. One caller said she had been told to 'stop being silly' by a member of staff when she reported being picked on, despite bruises to bear out her complaint.

In another example, a young boy had run away from his residential school and staff had used older residents to look for him. This had resulted in bullying. At the boy's request, ChildLine informed the social work department, who then investigated. The boy called later to say the situation had improved and thanked counsellors for their help.

Children had little confidence in the capacity of staff to stop bullying permanently in children's homes, because of inconsistencies in the way that individual staff members approached the problem. For example; one boy told us he felt safe most of the time except when a particular member of staff was on duty who 'sat in the office all shift' and was therefore not in a position to take any immediate action to combat disputes between residents.

Of callers in children's homes who said they were suffering bullying, all were in homes with 16 or more residents. Bearing in mind the greater difficulties of supervision, and heightened potential for dispute between residents in larger homes, it is likely that the size of the home is a contributory factor to this problem.

Physical abuse

Children reporting physical abuse (just over six per cent) were usually male callers. Their ages polarized at 8-9 and 15-16 years. Of these nine callers, a number began to suffer the abuse at home either as a result of parental separation or the death of one carer. Loss of different kinds appeared to act as a trigger for physical abuse. This is borne out by children calling about bereavement, who sometimes mentioned abusive behaviour by the remaining parent as a secondary problem. Callers also suffered physical abuse in their placements. For example:

> Vikky told the counsellor her foster mother was beginning to 'harass' her verbally and hit her. This abuse started when her foster parents split up. Her placement had been fine before then and she had lived there for over a year. She told the counsellor she felt like 'just packing my bag'.

Children told ChildLine about other physical abuse where carers were reported as being the perpetrators:

> David was in a children's home where he felt he was not being 'treated good' by staff. He suffered scratches and bruises from restraint and had been pulled upstairs by a staff member. He was contemplating running away when he called ChildLine, as he felt this was unjustified behaviour from staff which he could no longer endure

Much of this abuse was seen by the callers as either 'for no reason' or as a result of some disruptive act in which they had been involved, where staff reacted to them with physical force.

Some of the children placed in care initially because of physical abuse reported a continuation of this abuse on access visits to the perpetrator. They often did not tell anyone about this for fear either that disclosure might lead to more disruption in their lives, or that visits to relatives might be stopped completely.

Sexual abuse

Seventeen children (12 per cent of total callers) said they had suffered sexual abuse at some point. Half of these callers disclosed previous sexual abuse as secondary to more immediate problems. The abuse was often the reason the callers found themselves in care.

Nine children (just over six per cent of those calling) described sexual abuse as their main reason for calling. Most were female with an average age of 13. Just under half of the calls related to past rather than current abuse. Past abuse had usually occurred before admission into care or in previous placements, but continued to represent a significant problem for the caller. These children had often disclosed the abuse but found it difficult to explore their feelings and talk in any depth to the people around them.

Current abuse (ongoing sexual abuse) was reported by five children and occurred either on access visits to a relative or (in three cases) was perpetrated by a carer. Generally, these callers were reluctant to give sufficient information from which to draw conclusions or follow up.

In all, four callers had told no one of the abuse at the time of calling; two others had told only their best friends. The remaining children who called had told adults but reported experiencing responses they were not happy about. For instance:

> Rani was taken into care following abuse by her father. She felt isolated and unable to express her feelings to the people around her, saying she needed time to 'sort herself out' which was not being recognised. She was able to use ChildLine as a sounding board, testing out on the counsellor how she would approach staff and try to express how she felt.

Another caller was unhappy in her children's home but she felt unable to tell anyone in case she was moved to live with a family. She did not want this for fear of being abused again.

Family issues

Family members or general family problems were mentioned at some point in the majority of calls. Difficulties concerning relationships within the family were mentioned by 15 per cent of the total callers, either as a main or secondary problem. Many callers mentioned family problems as a reason for being placed in care. Most of these callers cited relationship difficulties with a specific family member as the root of the problem. Ten children also said that alcoholism or the ill-health of a main carer affected relationships within the family.

The family backgrounds from which children in the care system came varied widely, as did the amount of contact maintained with their family. Three callers specifically stated they had no contact with their family. Eight out of ten of total callers (114) indicated that they maintained some contact.

Thirty-five per cent of children maintained contact with mothers, compared with 17 per cent who had contact with fathers. Mothers were also most often cited as the 'person responsible' for the family problems. This could partly be a result of the fact that they are often the sole or main carers, having the most contact with, and responsibility for, their children.

Access to telephones

Ten per cent of the total callers expressly said that they had a continuing problem with restricted access to a telephone. Many also complained of little privacy, (for example, having to tell staff who they were calling) and restricted access at certain times. Telephones in children's homes are often in the staff office which children cannot use unsupervised. In foster families, telephones are likely to be in a family room or a 'public' part of the house.

To use the CIC Scotland Line, children need access to telephones. This is not always available or easy to achieve in foster and residential care. Many callers preferred to telephone from outside their placements to ensure they were not overheard. Telephone boxes, however, had their own problems and many callers had to end their calls because of a growing queue waiting to use the 'phone.

Leaving care

Thirteen percent of the total (18 callers) expressed specific concerns about leaving care. These callers ranged in age from 14 to 18 and the majority of calls were from children in residential care. The concerns they had were all based around issues of support. The following were the most frequently mentioned:

Practical help and advice

Overall, callers said they received little practical help and advice on leaving care. Many felt that decisions were taken 'at the last minute'. These decisions included pressure on them to return home rather than to move to independent living accommodation. Callers also felt they were expected to move before they were ready.

Callers reported being given inappropriate placements, such as being moved to a boarding house or lodgings with few facilities and rigid rules. For example:

> Fiona was placed in lodgings at 16. She felt the landlady was unreasonable, (for instance, insisting she was in by 10 pm). She also reported Fiona's movements to her social worker. Fiona requested a move on these grounds, but was not supported by her social worker.

Some callers felt that moves to independent placements were dependent on their compliance with staff's wishes. Their option of a place involved their taking on extra duties or attending access visits, with little room for negotiation.

Social and emotional support

Callers said they also experienced a lack of support in other areas. They often felt isolated and had no one with whom to talk or to share their fears of moving. It is difficult to establish a new network. Callers told us they felt unsupported in doing this or in learning to deal with new situations (for example, seeing parents unsupervised for the first time).

Several young people called who had recently moved from foster or residential care into independent placements and found that the move was not working out for them. At present, once a young person has left care (that is, the 'section' under which they were placed in care has been rescinded), the social work department is under no obligation to offer support on the same level as before. As a result, many young people could find themselves in the situation Sarah described:

> Sarah left care at 16 (before she felt ready) and moved to a flat on her own. After receiving little support she became lonely and distressed and felt like killing herself. She could not face going back there and eventually 'trashed' the flat so she would not have to live there.

Young people who find themselves in difficulties once they have left care have no way back into the care network, irrespective of the amount of time they have spent within it.

Employment

Another area about which young people were concerned was the lack of support, particularly from residential staff, in finding and maintaining employment. Examples included staff issuing travel expenses late and giving information on care status to perspective employers, (often jeopardising job prospects) without the young person's consent. Other problems included feeling isolated from staff and other residents once employment had begun: for example, not being included in activities within the placement.

Once young people move, it is difficult for key workers and staff to keep in touch. Pressures on their time make it hard to maintain a close relationship. The existing links with parents may be weak which can make moving more difficult.

As the Skinner Report[2] (1992) states:

> "For most people, parental support, however intermittent, carries on into their twenties. Young people and children in care also need this continuing support but often are not able to get it."

---

[2] *Another kind of home. A review of residential child care.* Angus Skinner, HMSO Edinburgh 1992.

Young people leaving care face many problems. In making the transition from care to independence without the conventional family help available to other young people, they need more rather than less practical and financial support. From the children's accounts, it appears that this is often not forthcoming.

Summary

This section has covered the issues most frequently mentioned by children calling the CIC Scotland Line. They span a wide range of aspects of the care system and some issues were brought up repeatedly. Fifty-two per cent of the total callers expressed a lack of confidence in residential staff or social workers. The reasons for this varied but in most cases related to instances where children felt they had been 'let down,' for example, carers not taking action on specific requests or not taking an interest in what children were doing or saying.

Sixty per cent of callers were unhappy with some aspect of the way they were cared for. The most common complaints were: no privacy, shared rooms, inflexible routines, exclusion from decisions and not being believed or listened to (for example, when they reported issues to staff). Underlying these complaints were feelings of powerlessness, having no control, a feeling that no one was interested. Anger and isolation show up as the two most common feelings callers experienced when trying to deal with their problems and the upheaval of moving through the care system.

Although some callers were confused or hazy about the intricacies of the process by which they arrived, or were remaining in care, they were, on the whole, extremely well-informed on the care system and their rights within it compared with their English and Welsh counterparts.

Scottish callers frequently mentioned visiting groups as sources of information: 'Who Cares?' Scotland in particular seem pro-active in visiting children and talking with them about their problems and their legal rights while in care.

While a generally negative perspective emerges from the nature and range of the issues about which children telephoned, it should be borne in mind that children call ChildLine for Children in Care Scotland when they are most distressed and in need of help. It follows that those having a more positive experience of the care system are less likely to be represented among those calling.

Face to face interviews with children in care

In Scotland, two regional authorities were approached and agreed to participate by inviting children in their care to be interviewed. All 17 children who took part had volunteered to talk to an interviewer about their experiences. All names and details have been altered in line with ChildLine's confidentiality policy (Appendix 3).

This part of the report offers an overall impression of the care system conveyed through the interviews. It must be remembered that the interviewees involved made up a small sample which should not be taken as representative of children in care as a whole. The children who took part were from a diverse group of placements including a hostel, children's homes, foster homes and a children's home with education on site. The youngest child interviewed was 12, the oldest 17. Thirteen were male and four were female. All had been in care longer than six months and many had stayed in the same placement for a number of years.

Admission into care/contact with family

Without exception, the reasons for coming into the care system stemmed from problems within the family. All children were still very much affected by this. Six children maintained regular contact with both parents while the others had either erratic visits or no contact. Regular family contact with aunts, uncles, grandparents, and so on, was, however, much more common. Some sets of parents had separated and now had new partners with whom the children did not get on, which made contact more difficult.

Most of those interviewed had brothers and sisters but few of them were in care. Of those who were, most were together, but there were exceptions, for example, where one of the children was in care under a 'section' related to criminal activity, which required placement in units of a specific nature.

Contact with siblings seemed more regular and informal than with other relatives, regardless of circumstance. Distance from the parental home was not a problem for most of the children, who were placed no further than five miles away. Two of the children who were in regular contact with parents had the longest journeys; however, their respective placements were intentionally outside their home area.

For a significant number of children the process of being admitted into care had been confusing. Children recalled the process of attending a Children's Hearing as intimidating, and said they had been scared to speak because, as one person put it: "What if I say something wrong and can't change it?" The 'panel' was however seen as a safe place to go in terms of getting help and, as with children calling the CIC Scotland Line, the children interviewed felt the Hearing system worked for them rather than against them. Nadia described her experience:

> At the first meeting, she was scared and her mum did all the talking. The members of the Children's Panel suggested she write them a letter setting out what she wanted to say for the next meeting – which she did. "My mum didn't have a chance..(to speak).. it gave me self-confidence to know someone was listening to me," said Nadia.

All children who mentioned going through the Hearing process thought overall it served to protect their interests and they had faith in the procedure. However, this was offset by the fear of attending and the officialdom and formality of the occasion.

Children sometimes found it difficult to reconcile their own perceptions and the reasons given by others for their being taken into care. They often started to tell the interviewers why they were in care by saying, "I think it's because..." indicating that they were not entirely clear. These children also cited the Children's Hearings as their main source of information on this decision. Children indicated that after the initial explanation they were given through the Hearing, the reasons why they had been removed from home were not discussed or explained in terms that made the decision clear to them. Although reasons for reception into care can be complex, the effect on children of not fully understanding why they are in this position is not confined to their immediate situation, but also adds to their uncertainty about the future. Many children were unhappy with this, unable to resolve their feelings and place their 'care history' into a present and future context without some support.

The details of the events leading up to the physical move into care were difficult for children to talk about. Most expressed a sense of relief at being admitted into care and distanced from the family conflict or point of stress. However, this also brought with it feelings of isolation, fear and confusion. Most were initially placed in children's homes which they found 'scary' but on the whole they thought staff and residents were kind. This had made settling in easier.

Moves into care were often handled badly, despite forward planning, as the following account from a young girl illustrates:

> "...the police came with a court order...'cause Mum refused...(to give her to social workers). They put me in a car and drove to the shop. They got me a drink and a bag of crisps, then took me to the new house."

A number of children felt angry and punished. "Why do I have to move here?" was a frequent feeling on being admitted into care. They felt singled out and removed as the 'problem' rather than as an individual needing help.

Rights and decisions

As was the case with children calling the CIC Scotland Line, all the children interviewed face to face had a ground knowledge of the care system in Scotland but were often unclear on how it related to them on a personal level. Most children could state what legal 'section' they were under; however, few could tell the interviewers what this meant or what other options there might be, indicating that insufficient time had been spent explaining the procedures and checking each child's understanding of these. Also, only a small number were able to say what was planned for them over the next year, despite most confirming the occurrence of reviews every six months. Children said they felt included in these meetings and were usually able to speak, yet did not feel they could challenge decisions made by the social work department.

Children interviewed in foster care were mostly there long-term and, through talking to their carers, had a better idea of their future plans than children in residential units. Most children had built up a knowledge of their rights and the procedures which affected them over the period of time since they entered the care system. A significant number said groups came to talk to them; usually these were locally-based youth groups and the 'Who Cares?' Scotland organisation. The latter in particular was seen as a useful point of reference. Two of the children were active in 'Who Cares?' groups concerned with gaining improvements for children in care. Most children voiced the idea that a good way to help would be for policy-makers and social work departments to talk to more children generally and set up meetings for children to discuss specific aspects of care and general problems. One young person said she had been looking forward to being interviewed by ChildLine Scotland specifically so that she could talk about her experiences and how she thought things could be improved.

Sources of support

When asked about support networks, all children identified a variety of people they would approach with a problem. Well-trusted 'best' friends and key workers were the first choices for most children in residential units. In foster care, either the foster mother or siblings were first choice. Social workers were not generally seen as likely people to talk to and were not highly regarded as good sources of support on a personal level. This was attributed to their often changing, having long periods of not visiting, being difficult to contact and spending little time with children when they did visit. Many children said they hardly knew their social workers and did not feel comfortable talking to them. One child who had approached her social worker with a problem described her as 'too judgmental'. This was also a view more generally reflected by callers to the CIC Scotland Line.

Children often preferred their key worker or foster parent to deal with the social work department on their behalf. These people were seen as highly valued sources of support and offered a link between 'official' and 'domestic' areas of being in care. Only one child did not have a key worker at the time of interview, and one was awaiting a replacement social worker.

Children generally felt detached from the language of the social work department and thought social workers talked at rather than to them. The children all had friends they saw regularly, often from their home area. Those in long-stay placements were planning to keep in touch on leaving, as they had established good friendships with other children in care.

Being in care

Almost all the children were in their first or second placement over a long period. The children were very clearly split into two groups: the majority who felt part of their unit and had built up a secure environment for themselves, and a small group who were unhappy and felt unsettled and isolated.

Most of the children interviewed did not want to return home, where this was an option. They believed nothing had changed in their family situations to ensure an end to the original problems and did not believe this was a realistic expectation.

The future

Care leavers are a particularly vulnerable group who often need additional support in making the transition to independent living and establishing a plan for the future. Of the children interviewed, many were thinking about their departure from care, but remained vague about what exactly they were entitled to and what their plans were.

Plans for the future (at age 30) were mainly based around having independence, owning a house and having a job. Only one child thought she would like to move away from Scotland permanently. A few wanted to travel. Both female and male interviewees (with one exception) wanted to pursue traditional career paths. The Army, joinery, painting and decorating were popular choices of job for males, and nursing and hairdressing for females.

The majority had made a decision not to move back home on leaving care. All wanted to maintain some degree of contact with their parents and/or family. A significant number made the point that this would be on their terms, reinforcing the feeling of control over their own lives that they would eventually like to achieve.

Summary

Dealing with family difficulties, and issues around maintaining contact with family and friends once in care, were problematic areas for all of the children interviewed. Links with family and friends were very important. Most of the children had an identified adult, (usually their key worker or foster mother) on whom they felt they could depend for support in negotiating their needs.

Although children had a working knowledge of the Scottish care system, they valued input from groups like 'Who Cares?' Scotland, who were seen as an independent source of information and advice. Expectations for the future centred on a desire for independence which they wanted to achieve through having a job and house of their own.

The children interviewed face to face in Scotland were, on the whole, comfortable with their placements and felt their move into care had been positive. They felt there was room for improvement in the support offered when entering and moving through the care system; in particular, they saw a need for clear and ongoing discussion about the reasons why they were in care and what future plans for them might be. The need for staff to include children in the decision-making process was also seen as a priority.

Conclusions

Many aspects of the lives of children in care in Scotland have been covered in this research. Children calling the CIC Scotland Line used it on many levels. They talked about a range of issues which were important to them, including problems with their placements, with family relationships, and physical and sexual abuse. While those interviewed face to face did appear to have less immediately troubling concerns and a more positive view of their lives in care than callers to the CIC Line, the analysis does suggest a common theme. Children want to talk about issues which appear fundamentally to stem from feelings of loss, powerlessness and isolation.

Entering a placement can be experienced as disruptive, even chaotic. In attempting to come to terms with their new environment, children need consistent and considerable support. They also need information on and access to a variety of support services which they can use flexibly. The same is true for young people leaving care who clearly feel themselves to be unsupported at a time of transition.

Consideration needs to be given to the means by which services for these children can be made available and better publicised, particularly in more sparsely populated areas where children are less likely to hear of them by word of mouth.

The research demonstrates that ChildLine Scotland can offer a level of support alongside that available from friends, family and professional agencies. This is especially true at points of transition or particular stress when children may need to speak to someone they regard as 'neutral', as a means of clarifying their feelings before deciding on a course of action. Children recently placed in care need to build relationships with people in their environment before they feel ready to trust them with their concerns.

The use of the CIC Scotland Line shows that children value having the space to talk without fear of repercussion. It can give children the confidence to try to tackle issues for themselves, thereby regaining some sense of control over their lives. The CIC Scotland Line took an intensive role with some callers, involving follow-up work through further calls. This meant that children could take time to decide whether they wanted intervention without feeling pushed into it before they were ready. Eight children were referred (with their consent) to a social work department, three having run away from their placements before contacting ChildLine.

The availability of this help is entirely dependent on children's access to a telephone which is, in turn, dependent on a number of variables. The location of the telephone, domestic arrangements where children live, the times available for using the 'phone and so on, all influence children's capacity to use the CIC Scotland Line. The research interviews showed that few of the homes involved gave children information about the Line or displayed posters, perhaps because of anxiety about the nature of the service or the response.

ChildLine Scotland is eager to work with regional authorities on special initiatives, particularly campaigning and development work, and to build partnerships so that children can reach us more easily. For example, Strathclyde Regional Council incorporated ChildLine's services into their

Children's Rights strategy and a special anti-bullying initiative, including a special Bullying Line run by ChildLine Scotland, was set up recently with Tayside Council.

The recommendations which follow are based on information taken directly from children in the Scottish care system. They are based on improving the responses to the emotional, social and physical needs of children in care to promote their wellbeing.

Recommendations

Introduction

These recommendations are made in the knowledge that there already exists potential for a great deal of change, both to children's legislation and to service provision, within Scotland. This includes the hoped-for Scottish Children's Bill and the changes implied by the Local Government etc. (Scotland) Bill.

Since 1988, there have been a number of reports on and inquiries into aspects of child care in Scotland, including those relating to Orkney, Fife, the Child Care Law Review, the Scottish Law Commission and the Family Law Report No. 135. Of more general relevance is the UN Convention on the Rights of the Child. The various reports generated in excess of 400 recommendations on Scottish child care. Most of these have been accepted in principle, and some have been acted upon. Many still await action or are dependent on new legislation. Some of the thinking underlying those recommendations is reflected and confirmed by ChildLine's research for *Time to listen.*

In the following recommendations, we propose steps which, while not directly related to the proposed changes in the Scottish system, could operate within a locally-based, well-structured Hearing system which has strong communication links with all involved professionals, and is therefore able to offer an effective service for children.

Because of the nature of the service that ChildLine offers, the recommendations inevitably focus on those issues children tell us about, which usually concern some aspect of their emotional needs. There is considerable evidence to suggest that these are frequently not being met. The recommendations are directed at social work departments and other professionals working in the field of child care.

1. Reception into care

The research findings show that children are often confused and upset when entering care and feel they have little control over the processes they undergo. They report a lack of support from adults at this point, which indicates that policies, practice and procedural guidelines need to be clearly spelt out and regularly reviewed.

A care plan, for both long and short-term placements, should be drawn up before a child enters care, or, where children come into care at short notice, as soon as possible. Care plans should be reviewed at regular intervals, with the child and his or her family.

2. Support in care

The research provides an insight into what children feel their needs are once placed in care. Children experience difficulties in adjusting to new settings. Contact with social workers often diminishes and feelings of isolation and frustration are common. This is compounded by social workers not spending enough time with children on visits, which adds to the child's feeling of lack of control and understanding of their situation.

Children in foster care can be more isolated. They may have less contact with peers and are less likely to be aware of services available to them. This could be due to a lack of independent information or the perception that placement in a foster home is not really 'being in care'. Abuse by other residents in the foster home is also less likely to be revealed if children do not have the opportunity to speak to workers alone for any length of time.

i) Children should be encouraged to take an active part in day to day planning in their placements, such as participating in buying food, household care, organising outings, and so on. The needs of children to have their own space, privacy, and a say in the way they live should be respected.

ii) Continuing a relationship with a young person in care should be given a higher status when social work case-loads are prioritised. This is difficult for many workers to achieve because of pressures on time and volume of work.

iii) Social workers need to spend time with children on visits to placements. At least some of this time should be spent in private with the child, particularly in foster care.

3. Abused children in care

The research shows that, where children have been abused, the type of placement selected is particularly important. Some callers were afraid of being placed with a small family, for fear of being abused again. Placing children in residential homes in these circumstances might be a positive alternative.

Measures to reduce the risks of abuse to children should be considered as a matter of urgency. They include more frequent visits from social workers; establishing and legitimising children's access to other professionals and to informal care networks; and further training for all levels of staff in the development of assessment skills for judging the suitability of placements.

4. Bullying

The research shows that bullying is a common problem for children and that it is more likely to occur in larger establishments. Regional authorities are currently developing small residential care units in line with the recommendations of previous research findings. Skinner and Utting[3] among others, suggest a maximum number of residents of

---

3 *Another kind of home. A review of residential care.* Angus Skinner, HMSO Edinburgh 1992; Children in the public care. *A review of residential child care.* Sir William Utting, HMSO 1991.

between eight and 12 children, depending on age and needs. ChildLine's findings indicate that these smaller units do offer children a greater sense of security. They also enable staff to develop a more coherent approach for dealing with problems such as bullying.

i) The practice of allocating secondary key workers could be more widely used in larger units to offer children a greater level of continuity and support.

ii) Each authority should formulate an effective anti-bullying policy. This would enable staff to develop a more consistent approach to dealing with bullying. In implementing this, staff should involve other children, consulting them on an ongoing basis about ways of tackling bullying and other problems.

5. Rights and decisions

Children in care need to know what choices are open to them and what rights they have. They need this information presented to them in clear, understandable form. Skinner, (in recommendation 2 of his report) states that as often as possible children's preferences (of placement,) should be followed. But children tell us that those who make the important decisions about their lives are not listening to them. The fact that this continues to be the case is of serious concern and needs to be addressed.

The research also shows that children are not always able to use a telephone, or to do so in private. The location and times available for some children were unreasonable and not readily negotiable.

i) Children should be given the opportunity to have their views acknowledged, taken seriously and acted upon where appropriate. Where action is not possible, it is important to spend time with the child, discussing why this is the case. In these circumstances staff need to check how the child feels and how the child can be supported.

ii) Children in care should be able to make a complaint without the knowledge of staff or foster carers, as should their family. (Skinner Report, recommendation 17.). Social workers and others should take children's complaints seriously and the existence of complaints procedures, children's rights officers, children's charters and strategies and external support agencies that can help children should all be well-publicised.

iii) Children should have free and appropriate access to a telephone, in private.

6. Support networks

The findings indicate that maintaining links between children in care and their family can be very difficult. As Skinner recommends, parents should be involved as much as possible:

"Research indicates very clearly that where strong family links are maintained there is a greater likelihood of the child in care returning home" (3.61 P59) He goes on to say: "Parents are as likely to need help and support...as are their children and it is important their needs are not neglected; there may well be a need for emotional support" (3.65 P59).

i) Professional services both inside and outside the social work department should be available to help children to maintain relationships with their family and friends while they are in care.

ii) Children's informal support networks, such as friends and adults who are not relatives, should be recognised and involved in planning. For instance, they should be included when access visits to family are planned and should be allowed to accompany children to meetings at the child's request. This should be part of the wider strategy to enable children to have their views heard.

7. Leaving care

The findings demonstrate that children who will not be returning home need to know what options are available and to have their views properly considered. The Review of Child Care Law[4] made

[4] *(Review of Child Care Law in Scotland.* The Scottish Office 1990 HMSO Edinburgh)

recommendations for after-care which were echoed in the Skinner Report. These were based on each region having a range of facilities to offer children leaving care, including adequate support and access to practical advice and information. The Review also recommends that these facilities should be available, if necessary, until the young person is 21.

At present, once a legal requirement is removed, (that is, the legal 'section' a child is under while in care) even children who are only 16 are unable to fall back on the system they have recently left. So they often find themselves with little support and no rights to return to a more supportive environment.

An effective 'safety net' should be developed for young people who need more time to adjust to leaving care.

8. Independent developments

In the course of the research children indicated that they sometimes found it difficult to explain themselves, (to workers, at Hearings, to their parents.) Children interviewed also suggested setting up meetings with policy-makers and social work department representatives to discuss specific aspects of care and issues of general concern to them. These and other ways of facilitating children's communication (for instance, letters, tapes, being accompanied by a friend to Hearings/reviews for moral support) all help to ensure that children are heard. Further work needs to be undertaken in this area with a specific brief to advocate on children's behalf (which can differ from interventions in their 'best interests'.)

i) Social work departments should strengthen their links with external organisations. In particular, they should continue to work with 'Who Cares?' Scotland,[5] which already has experience of organising conferences for children.

---

[5] Alongside the Scottish Child Law Centre and ChildLine Scotland, 'Who Cares?' was commissioned to undertake a consultation exercise with young people, which was used as a basis for informing the preparation of the White Paper *Scotland's children*. These organisations have established a positive image with the young people they involve.

ii) Individuals and groups placed outside the social work department, but recognised within it, should be available for children to talk to at their request, such as 'Who Cares?' Scotland.

iii) In order to help young people become more confident about speaking out and also to enable them to be involved in working out difficulties within their care settings, group discussion and involvement should be encouraged as a regular feature. This is likely to require additional training for staff.

BIBLIOGRAPHY

Audit Commission (1994), *Seen but not heard*, HMSO
Berridge D & Cleaver H (1987), *Foster home breakdown*, Basil Blackwell
Beitchman et al (1992) *A review of the long-term effects of sexual abuse* in *Child abuse and neglect*, Vol 16, p101-115, USA.
Children Act (1989), London, HMSO.
Children's Rights Development Unit (1993), *Day to day care of children*
Department of Health (1989), *The care of children: Principles and practice in regulations and guidance.*
Department of Health (1991), *Regulations and guidance to the Children Act, Vol 2*, HMSO
Department of Health and Social Security (1985), *Social work decisions in child care. Recent research findings and their implications.*
Finkelhor D. & Browne A. *Initial and long-term effects: A conceptual framework* in Finkelhor D (1986) *A source book on child sexual abuse*, Sage.
Fromuth M E (1986), *The relationship of childhood sexual abuse with later psychological and sexual adjustment in a sample of college women* in *Child abuse and neglect*, Vol 10, p5-15, USA.
Howard League for Penal Reform (1993), *Young and in trouble.*
Jackson S (1989) *Education of Children in Care* in *Child Care Research, Policy and Practice*, Ed. Kahan B, The Open University
Meir Gottesmann, eds. (1991), *Residential child care, an international reader.* Whitting and Birch Ltd.
NCH Action for Children (1993), *A Lost Generation?*
NSPCC (1992), *Experience of child abuse in residential care and educational placements.*
Rowe J. & Lambert L. (1973), *Children who wait.* Association of British Adoption Agencies.
Southampton University (1993), *Answering Back*, Dolphin Project.
Scottish Office (1993), *Proposals for child care policy and law.* HMSO
Scottish Office (1990), *Review of child care law in Scotland.* HMSO Edinburgh.
Skinner A, Scottish Office (1992), *Another kind of home: A review of residential child care.* HMSO
Stevenson D. (1968), *Reception into care; the meaning for all concerned. Children in Care.* Longman.
Utting W, (1991), *Children in the public care A review of residential child care.* HMSO
Warner N, (1992) *Choosing with care, Report of the committee of enquiry into the selection, development and management of staff in children's homes.* HMSO
Whittaker *et al* (1991), *Patterns and outcomes in child placement.* HMSO
Who Cares? Scotland 1993 *Annual Report.*

APPENDIX 1

The research approach

The research aimed to provide information about the problems and concerns of children in public care and the sources of support available to them through an analysis of the records of counselling calls to ChildLine for Children in Care, supplemented by in-depth, face to face interviews with a group of children currently in public care.

Analysis of calls

Between 14th October 1992 and 31st March 1993, the ChildLine for Children in Care (CIC) Line received 9,483 total calls, 8,657 from England and Wales and 826 from Scotland. From these calls, 676 children were counselled and 45 adults were advised. As several children rang back for follow-up counselling, some more than once, the total number of 'counselling exchanges' for children was around 1,100 in England and Wales and 220 in Scotland.

The discrepancy between the total calls figure and the number of counselling exchanges is not unusual for ChildLine. This is because we receive a large number of calls where children are testing out the nature of the service, the confidentiality policy, and their own ability to speak about their problems. Children may have great difficulty in beginning to speak about problems such as abuse, and will sometimes call several times, asking only brief questions. Such exchanges are not regarded as counselling. On average, eight to ten per cent of all calls made to ChildLine will result in a child being counselled.

Counselling calls were recorded under a series of headings. The most important of these (for research purposes) is the 'main problem' category. This is used to indicate the main reason for contacting the Line, as identified by the caller. Other examples include 'type of placement' and 'reasons for being in care'. Specific categories were identified before the lines opened and each casenote which contained the relevant information was coded accordingly. A number of issues inevitably emerged from the records which had not been anticipated in the pre-coding system. These issues were post-coded.

The analysis of counselling records took the form of a detailed review of individual case-notes; checking the accuracy and consistency of the pre-coded information and recording any issues for post-coding. Most of the issues identified in the post-coding exercise were not quantifiable; instead the code operated as a tag, identifying those cases which contained information on a common issue or theme.

Face to face interviews with young people

Sixty three children, in seven local authority areas in England and Wales and two regional council areas in Scotland, were interviewed face to face. They included children in both foster care and various types of residential placement (both short-term and long-term). Because of limits on time, it was decided that the interviews would not include children in specialist provision, notably psychiatric units, special needs provision and 'secure' accommodation.

The interviews were semi-structured, using an interview schedule (see Appendix 2) as a guide to areas of interest, but allowing interviewers to conduct the interview informally. The conversational format facilitated exploration of areas which children themselves felt were important to discuss.

The process of identifying children for interview varied across the areas. Some local authorities in England and Wales and regional councils in Scotland wrote to all children for whom they cared, asking them if they would like to participate. Others targeted children in specific districts to make the task more manageable. Two local authorities in England and Wales identified specific homes or children they thought might agree to be interviewed.

All the children approached were given an information pack which included a sheet outlining the areas to be covered by the interview questions (see Appendix 3). Children were only interviewed if they had explicitly agreed, having been made aware of the broad areas for discussion.

The interviewers all had experience of direct work with children. Where possible, children's requests to be interviewed by, for example, a black person or a woman were met. Interviewers were trained in appropriate interview techniques, and particular attention was given to strategies to support children who might become distressed during the interview. The interviewers themselves were supported by a network of counselling and research staff.

APPENDIX 2

INTERVIEW SCHEDULE

Residential/foster care

INTRODUCTION

Introduction to the interview

Establishing terms/format of the interview.

Outline confidentiality policy

Any questions?

IN CARE – THE HOME

What is it like being in care?

Prompts

What is the best thing about being in care?

What is the worst thing about being in care?

What is it like living here?

What do you think of the staff (your foster parents)?

What do you think of the other children (foster siblings)?

What do you think about the facilities? (eg. bedrooms, living area, meals etc)

What to do think about the rules you live by?

If you were in charge of the home would you make any changes to how it is run? (Foster – If you could, would you make any changes to the way you live?

PLACEMENTS

When did you first come into care? (Do you know why?)

Do you remember what you thought about coming into care?

Have you had any other placements?

Prompts

(If Yes,) Which did you like and why?
Which did you dislike and why?

Why did you change placements?

SOCIAL WORKERS/KEY WORKER

What do you think of your social worker?

What do you think of your key worker/foster parent?

Prompts

How often do you see your social worker/key worker?

What sorts of things do you talk about?

Do you find his/her visits helpful?

SUPPORT SOURCES

If you have a problem/worry do you usually talk to someone about it? (Who & Why?)

Prompts

Would you be able to talk to your social worker about any problems/worries? (What sort of probs)

Is there anyone in your family you can talk to about problems/worries? (Who and what sorts of probs)

Would you be able to talk to anyone at school about problems/worries? (Who and what sort of probs)

Can you talk to staff in the home/foster parent about problems/worries? (Who and what sort?)

Have you other friends in home or elsewhere you can talk to? (What sort of probs)

If you had a very serious problem who do you think you would talk to about it?

Do you have access to a telephone where you could make a private call? (Where is it, in the home, is it used heavily)

Have you heard of the ChildLine for Children in Care Line? (What do you think of the idea? What sorts of problems do you think they deal with?)

FAMILY AND HOME

Are you still in touch with any of your relatives?

Prompts

Where do most of your family live? (How far is this?)

Who lives at home now?

Who are you closest to and why? How often do you see them?

Do you have any brothers/sisters – are they in care? Do you see them? How often?

LEISURE

What do you do in your spare time?

Prompts

Do you spend spare time with the staff at the home (fosterparents)?

With the other residents (foster siblings)?

With relatives (NB. contact with family)

SCHOOL

Are you at school?

What do you like about it? What do you dislike about it?

Prompts

Did you change schools when you came into care?

How do you get on with the other kids at school?

Do you like the teachers/staff?

What do you hope to achieve at school?

FUTURE

When you think about the future, what are you looking forward to?

Prompts

How do you think you'l feel when you leave care?

What do you hope to be doing when you are about 30 yrs old?

PERSONAL IDENTITY/DETAILS

How would you describe yourself? (eg. Interviewer describe self)

Large / small

Male / female

I describe myself as 'ethnic origin', what about you?

How old do you say you are?

How old are you? (change as appropriate to interviewer/age of child)

OTHER (NB. Ask at end of interview)

Is there anything else you would like to tell me about yourself or your life in care that we haven't covered?

Which of the things we have talked about is most important to you?

ENDING

Summary of what discussed

How did you find the interview?

How do you feel? (explain CIC and other counselling back-up)

Explain what happens to information and restate confidentiality.

Are there any questions you would like to ask me?

APPENDIX 3

INFORMATION LEAFLET FOR POTENTIAL INTERVIEWEES

ChildLine is doing some research on being in care. You have been asked if you would like to take part by being interviewed. But, before you decide, we would like you to know what would happen at the interview.

- The interview will be confidential – that means whatever you say is just between you and ChildLine, unless you want us to talk to somebody for you, or if your life is in danger.

- The interviewer will be a ChildLine worker but will NOT be a counsellor (if you feel you would like to talk to a counsellor we can put you in touch with one).

- You do not have to answer all the questions in the interview. If there is a question you do not want to answer you can say so and that will be fine. You can also stop the interview if you decide you do not want to go on.

- The interviewer would like to know about your views and thoughts on:

    WHERE YOU LIVE

    OTHER PLACEMENTS YOU HAVE HAD

    YOUR SOCIAL WORKER/KEY WORKER

    WHERE YOU GET HELP WITH PROBLEMS

    FAMILY AND HOME

    LEISURE INTERESTS

EXPERIENCES AT SCHOOL

CHILDLINE FOR CHILDREN IN CARE (The special telephone helpline ChildLine is running)

YOUR HOPES AND PLANS FOR THE FUTURE

SOME PERSONAL DETAILS – LIKE YOUR AGE

The interview will be taped to help us write up the research, but the tape will also be confidential. Your interview will be wiped off when the research project is finished.

ChildLine will write a report on the research and you will get a free copy when it has been finished. The report will not have any personal details or information about you from which you can be recognised.

The information you give us will be kept confidential and no names will be kept in our records of the research work.

We very much hope you will want to be part of this work.

The report will be a way of putting forward your views and those of other children who are being looked after by local authorities.

APPENDIX 4

ChildLine's confidentiality policy

1   Confidentiality resides in ChildLine as an Agency, rather than in individual employees or volunteers.

2   ChildLine offers a confidential counselling service to children and young people. A child telephoning or writing must be assured that the information s/he has given is confidential and it will not be divulged to any person outside ChildLine.

3   The only exception when the contract of confidentiality can be broken is when the child is perceived to be in a dangerous/life-threatening situation. However, there must always be an **informed** judgment as to whether the child can give realistic consent to act on his/her behalf.

In such a situation (i.e. where a child is perceived to be at risk and is withholding permission for ChildLine to take action) before confidentiality is broken the counsellor must:

Confer with a Supervisor
(if possible and appropriate)
Share with the caller/writer the action that ChildLine intends to take

4   No information concerning a caller/writer can be divulged to outside parties without the permission of the caller and/or the knowledge and permission of a senior manager.

5   Any information from any source which gives rise to concern for the safety or wellbeing of a child or young person, directly or indirectly, should be made known to a senior manager immediately.

NB: The above policy will also relate to interviews carried out on ChildLine's behalf.∆

APPENDIX 5

Breakdown of calls to the CIC Line from Children in foster care in England and Wales, Oct. '92 to March '93

MAIN PROBLEMS OF CHILDREN IN FOSTER CARE IN ENGLAND & WALES	Number of Female Children	Number of Male Children	Total Children	% Total
SEXUAL ABUSE	23	1	24	15
PHYSICAL ABUSE	18	2	20	12
IN CARE	12	2	14	9
DECISION MAKING	10	3	13	8
FAMILY RELATIONSHIP PROBLEMS	12	0	12	7.5
RUNAWAY	8	3	11<	7
LIVING CONDITIONS	6	4<	10	6
PREGNANCY	10	0<	10	6
DISLIKE OF PLACEMENT	9	0	9	6
NON SPECIFIC ABUSE	5	0	5	3
LEGAL	2	2	4	2
FACTS OF LIFE	3	0	3	2
HEALTH	3	0	3	2
PAST SEXUAL ABUSE	3	0	3	2
BULLYING	0	2	2	1.5
OTHER PROBLEMS	2	1	3	1.5
REQUEST FOR RESOURCES	1	1	2	1.5
SANCTIONS	2	0	2	1.5
BEREAVEMENT	1	0	1	.5
COMPLAINTS	1	0	1	.5
DOMESTIC VIOLENCE	1	0	1	.5
LONELINESS	1	0	1	.5
PROBLEM FRIENDS	1	0	1	.5
RACISM	1	0	1	.5
SCHOOL PROBLEM	1	0	1	.5
SELF HARM	1	0	1	.5
SEXUALITY	1	0	1	.5
SMOKING	1	0	1	.5
THIRD PARTY	1	0	1	.5
VIOLENCE IN CARE	1	0	1	.5
TOTALS	141	21	162	100

APPENDIX 6

Breakdown of calls to the CIC Line from Children in residential care in England and Wales, Oct. '92 to March '93

MAIN PROBLEMS OF CHILDREN IN RESIDENTIAL CARE IN ENGLAND & WALES	Number of Female Children	Number of Male Children	Total Children	% Total
BULLYING	13	14	27	10
SEXUAL ABUSE	20	5	25	9
BEING IN CARE	18	4	22	8
RUNAWAY	17	5	22	8
DECISION-MAKING	15	2	17	6
DISSATISFIED WITH PLACEMENT	12	3	15	5
PREGNANCY	15	0	15	5
VIOLENCE IN CARE	11	4	15	5
FAMILY RELATIONSHIP PROBLEMS	10	3	13	5
SANCTIONS	8	4	12	4
PAST SEXUAL ABUSE	11	1	12	4
PHYSICAL ABUSE	7	5	12	4
LIVING CONDITIONS	7	4	11	4
THIRD PARTY	8	1	9	3
REQUEST FOR RESOURCES	4	3	7	3
LONELINESS	6	0	6	2
LEGAL	4	1	5	2
PARTNER RELATIONSHIP PROBLEMS	4	0	4	1.5
BEREAVEMENT	2	1	3	1
COMPLAINTS	2	1	3	1
DRUG ABUSE	0	3	3	1
HEALTH	3	0	3	1
RISK OF ABUSE	3	0	3	1
SEXUALITY	3	0	3	1
OTHER	3	0	3	1
PROBLEM FRIENDS	2	0	2	1
SUICIDE	2	0	2	1
EMOTIONAL ABUSE	0	1	2	.5
HOMELESSNESS	0	1	1	.5
OFFENDING	0	1	1	.5
SCHOOL PROBLEM	0	1	1	.5
TOTALS	210	68	278	100

APPENDIX 7

Main problems of children who called the CIC Scotland line, Oct. '92 - March '93

MAIN PROBLEMS CIC SCOTLAND	FC	MC	TOTAL
TOTAL IN CARE: RELATED PROBLEMS	10	9	19
RUNAWAY: RELATED PROBLEMS	7	11	18
DECISION MAKING	9	4	13
BULLYING	8	3	11
FAMILY RELATIONSHIP PROBLEMS	9	1	10
PHYSICAL ABUSE	2	7	9
SEXUAL ABUSE	7	2	9
THIRD PARTY	5	1	6
OTHER	3	2	5
PREGNANCY	4	1	5
RISK OF ABUSE: BEING FOLLOWED	3	2	5
REQUEST FOR RESOURCES	2	2	4
SCHOOL PROBLEM	2	2	4
DRUG ABUSE	3	1	4
SEXUALITY, FACTS OF LIFE	1	3	4
LEGAL PROBLEMS	2	1	3
BEREAVEMENT	1	0	1
HEALTH	1	0	1
HOMELESSNESS	1	0	1
LONELINESS	1	0	1
ABUSE: NON-SPECIFIC	2	0	2
PARTNER RELATIONSHIP	0	1	1
RACISM	0	1	1
TOTAL	83	54	137

Of those children who said where they were living, 65 (55%) were in childrn's homes and 24 (20%) in foster care.

NOTE:

In Appendices 5, 6 and 7, OTHER includes calls on individual subjects not frequent enough to display as separate statistics. THIRD PARTY denotes calls relating to other people.